15 Easy Lessons
That Build Basic Writing Skills
in Grades K-2

by Mary Rose

SCHOLASTIC
PROFESSIONAL BOOKS

NEW YORK • TORONTO • LONDON • AUCKLAND • SYDNEY
MEXICO CITY • NEW DELHI • HONG KONG • BUENOS AIRES

DEDICATION

Dedicated to my Marshall University supervising teacher in 1971,
Mrs. Claire Cubby, second grade teacher (retired) at
Geneva Kent Elementary School, Huntington, W. Va.

ACKNOWLEDGMENTS

Special thanks go to Mrs. Donna Jean Smith, Mrs. Susan Kinney,
Mr. John Rowland, Mr. Roy Arenth and Dr. Joseph Joyner of
Orange County (Orlando, Florida) Public Schools, and to Terry
Cooper, Wendy Murray, Joanna Davis-Swing, Deborah Dragovic,
and Jackie Swensen of Scholastic.

Cover design by Weaver Design
Cover photo by Vicky Kasala
Interior design by Solutions by Design, Inc.
Interior photos by Tom and Mary Rose

ISBN 0-439-27163-0

Table of Contents

Foreword

"I wish our lower grades were doing more with writing."

"We never had a writing class in college. I don't know where to begin!"

"I am not happy with the quality of my students' journal writing."

"How much modeling should I do?"

"Should I still be writing whole-class experience stories in the second grade?"

"We cannot wait until fourth grade to start preparing students for state writing assessments."

These are just a few of the comments and questions I hear as I travel from school to school, working with teachers of grades K-5 to improve their students' scores on state writing assessments. It is because of these many conversations and concerns that I have decided to write this book.

My 20 years of teaching kindergarten and first grade have given me a clear understanding of what young children can do as writers. In my recent experience as a fourth-grade teacher, I learned the importance of helping children develop their writing skills early on—before they enter a grade in which they will be tested. I believe it is primary teachers' responsibility to give their students a strong foundation for their futures as writers—not just for the sake of testing.

All children need is to understand the mechanics of writing and how to organize their thoughts. Possessing solid writing skills will help them throughout their school lives, with report writing, creative writing, and responses to reading. These lessons should be helpful to any teacher who wishes to help budding writers work on the basics and who is eager to see progress in students' writing.

Thanks for all of your hard work in helping young children to become confident writers!

Mary Rose

Introduction

As students move from the primary to intermediate grades, they are asked to demonstrate their learning by writing in a variety of genres, from book reports, science-lab journals, and friendly letters to state performance assessments. The benefit of having students enter the third and fourth grades with the skills described in this book cannot be overstated. Far too often, teachers in the intermediate grades are supposed to be teaching students to write a research paper and instead must teach them how to write a sentence! The lessons presented here should take some of the mystery out of writing, enabling most students to become focused, organized writers who can skillfully support their main ideas and edit their work.

Moreover, these lessons will prepare students for the high-stakes tests they will face later in their academic careers. State writing assessments are usually administered in grades 3, 4, or 5, and more and more states are testing students across all disciplines. Many state tests ask students to compose essays for the writing portion and to explain—in writing—content-area concepts. For instance, students may be asked to demonstrate understanding of a reading passage or a mathematical problem by writing paragraphs discussing the passage or explaining how the problem was solved. Thus, competence in written expression no longer means just getting a good score on the state writing assessment—it has become an essential tool to pass tests in reading and math, as well. These are performance assessments. While multiple-choice questions still exist, they are no longer the mainstay on these tests. Thirty-eight states currently have a performance-based writing assessment, and more are in development.

Teachers in the grades where these tests are administered feel mounting pressure to ensure that their students do well. After all, test scores can determine ratings of and funding for a school, a student's passing or failure of a grade level, and even teacher salaries and bonuses. For all of these reasons and more, we cannot wait until students reach the third or fourth grade to begin teaching writing techniques.

The Basic Skills

It's critical to remember that there are four specific traits that characterize strong writing. We must teach these to students, to give them the tools they need to write well. In addition, these are the very criteria by which student writing is judged on assessments.

The main categories are *focus, organization, support,* and *conventions of print*:

Focus refers to the writer's ability to clearly address the topic throughout the essay. (Other terms for focus are *purpose, subject, key event,* and *main event*.)

Organization is the presentation of information in logical order, with an appropriate introduction and conclusion. (Other terms for organization are *format, plan,* or *method*.)

Support refers to all of the information that helps to express the main idea or ideas. Under support we find other elements of writing such as *tone, voice, word choice, elaboration, extensions, details,* and *description*.

Conventions of print is a broad term referring to all rules of punctuation, grammar, paragraphing, and so on that serve to make writing completely clear to the reader. (Related terms for conventions of print are *mechanics* and *usage*.)

Even in the earliest grades, we can model these elements in developmentally appropriate ways—we can teach children their value from the very first days of kindergarten! When you list events planned for the day or create a Morning Message to the class, you are modeling writing skills. You are demonstrating all of the print conventions and showing children how to cluster like ideas in a piece—the beginning of paragraphing. If you reread the message and add a title, you provide a focus for the just-completed text—and help students think about main idea.

If you do all of this, by the time it's their turn to write, children will have had considerable exposure to writing techniques (and they will have observed a proficient writer—you—at work). By the first grade, students will be ready to write about an assigned topic. They will understand that a good essay for them will have at least five sentences, the first and last being the introduction and the closing. Later in the year, even kindergartners can learn to revise and edit their work, correcting errors, and adding short extensions to further explain their topic sentences and to correct errors.

Sound too difficult? Read on. Students can even learn to use graphic organizers in the first grade! With consistent modeling and frequent discussions about writing, primary students can tackle beginning writing tasks with confidence.

How This Book is Organized

This book presents a series of 15 lessons, arranged in order of increasing difficulty. I have not attached grade levels to them, because the writing instruction your students need depends on their past experience and current abilities—not their grade level. Begin where your students need you to, and adapt as you see fit.

Each lesson has a particular focus and builds skills related to future writing assessments. These are highlighted at the beginning of each lesson so you can choose what you need to meet your objectives. However, keep in mind that state writing standards for grades K-2 are vague or nonexistent; I have merely included attainable and relevant goals for these young writers that they can build on in later grades.

CHAPTER 1

Good Morning Greetings

After the Pledge of Allegiance, calendar activities, and a greeting song, many primary-grade teachers move into a shared writing activity such as a Good Morning Greeting or Morning Message. Students gather on the floor and discuss the day's schedule, upcoming plans, and important classroom events. As students suggest ideas or sentences, the teacher writes these on chart paper, the chalkboard, or a white board. While some teachers prepare the greeting or message before students arrive, I find it's much more effective as a modeling tool if students see me write and hear me thinking about what I'm writing.

Modeling Writing Skills With Good Morning Greetings

Through your Good Morning Greeting, you can model correct spelling, punctuation, and grammar, providing students with their first glimpse of "talk written down." But these messages can provide far more than that. Writing this daily text is a prime opportunity to discuss the writing process, demonstrate generating and organizing ideas, model editing techniques, and invite student participation in the composing process. In other words, Good Morning Greetings can demonstrate kindergarten and first-grade versions of most of the elements of good writing that students at the fourth- or fifth-grade level are expected to include in their writing.

Over the course of the school year, the lessons and activities that grow from the Good Morning Greetings evolve and reflect what students have learned about writing. The daily text can reinforce past lessons and introduce new ideas. See the suggestions that follow to get the most out of your Good Morning Greetings.

Tips for Success

※ **Keep all of your Good Morning Greetings on chart paper.** They can remain in a tablet or be torn out and displayed. Remember to date each day's page. These collected greetings become a resource for activities later in this book and serve as a wonderful resource for celebrating events such as the 50th or 100th day of school.

※ **Occasionally reread Morning Messages about previous events.** This activity helps students understand the passage of time and enjoy remembering important classroom events, such as when the hamster had babies, when Joey was a new student, and when the class got a new computer.

※ **Change the color of marker used with each new month.** That makes it easy to spot greetings that were written with October Orange, December Green, February Red, or April Violet. If they are torn out and displayed, use a large clip or skirt hanger to keep monthly messages together.

※ **Leave a couple of lines between topic sentences students suggest.** Students often give their ideas for the Morning Message in random order. Leaving space as you write gives you room to add to an idea someone has already introduced.

For example, a child might say, "Today we will visit the library," which you transcribe. The rest of the class might mention lunch, the weather, or the new computer before another child interjects that the class will get to check out books from the library. If you have left a space beside or below the initial sentence about visiting the library, there is room to go back to add the sentence about checking out books.

As simple as this might seem, it is powerful in its effect, because it establishes putting "like" subjects together and introduces the concept of paragraphing. It also helps children see that adding to one's writing—even adding an entire sentence, if necessary—is not a bad thing; the teacher does it all the time! Be sure to reread the finished greeting so the students can hear how all the sentences come together.

※ **Vary the kinds of Morning Messages you write.** Include both narrative and expository messages. For narratives, students might tell a story about a new student's arrival or the addition of a classroom pet. For an expository message, students could explain how to do something, such as carve a pumpkin or create clay animals, or discuss reasons for something, such as why they are looking forward to a classroom visitor or a field trip.

❋ **Use a pointer to point to each word as you read the Morning Message out loud.** Pointing as you read aloud reinforces the left-to-right-top-to-bottom-return-sweep motion of reading. As you read aloud this way every day, students' eyes and brains become accustomed to this familiar movement.

This action also helps children separate what they hear into meaningful units—words. If you have ever had a child write about a friend who came over "daspendanit" (to spend the night), you can see the value of this activity. Young children often have a concept of something but think it's an expression as opposed to distinct words. In addition, since your greetings will use some of the same words each day, students will begin to develop their sight-word vocabulary.

You can also use your pointer to emphasize the job of the period to stop the reading and have fun as you overemphasize the pause between sentences! (See Lesson 3, page 24.)

Some Pointers on Pointers

To vary the read-aloud experience, collect many pointers such as magic wands, candy canes, rulers, shamrocks on a stick, small flags, and so on. Keep these in a can near the chart, and let students choose a pointer and lead the reading. Have these available during class center time, too. Students will often "play school" by pointing and rereading even when the teacher is not listening.

❋ **Model effective closing paragraphs.**
One way to do this is to "write in a circle," which means you simply choose one word from the introduction and use it in the closing. Teaching a child to do this is much easier than asking her to "restate the prompt" or to tie up the ending in any other way. Almost any child can use this circle writing to make a piece seem whole and complete. Look at the samples in Lessons 1, 2, and 4 to identify the word from the introductory paragraph that is repeated in the closing.

❋ **Conduct interactive lessons with the completed charts.** You have worked a long time to create these charts, so use them for several lessons. For example, have students find all of the words that say "we" or all of the words that mean numbers. Count the numbers of periods and capital letters. Refer to these charts when instructing students about indenting or about the correct way to form letters. These kinds of lessons are not only the foundations for future writing activities, but they also help the child in the process of learning to read.

In later chapters, I share lessons that invite students to do more and more independent writing; by the end of this book, the lessons are geared for students at a second-grade level. They guide students to write a story about an event, write an essay explaining their thinking, or write a report about something they have learned. Learning to write effectively is a long, arduous process and one that many adults have not yet mastered. With a lot of practice and an eye toward future expectations in writing, we can begin to teach children to excel at written expression.

Using a Format for Good Morning Greetings

Skill Focus: *Including an Introduction, Body, and Closing*

CONNECTION TO WRITING ASSESSMENTS . . . .
- ❈ Demonstrates use of organizational plan.
- ❈ Models conventions of print.

At the beginning of kindergarten, it is a good idea to have a predictable format for each day's Good Morning Greeting. Children will know what to expect each day, and they can even begin to plan ahead for what their contribution might be. Repeating the same opening and key phrases, such as "Good morning, boys and girls" or "Today is the _____ day of school," also helps young readers recognize basic words.

In intermediate grades, students are required to demonstrate an organizational plan in their writing, including an introduction, a body and a closing. We can introduce this idea in the primary grades by talking about introductions, body paragraphs, and closings in our Good Morning Greetings. While we do not want any child to be locked into prescriptive writing forever, it is a valid way to begin teaching a child basic techniques such as clustering like ideas together (paragraphing), getting events in order (sequencing), and including words or phrases in the conclusion that relate to the introduction (writing in a circle).

Presenting the Lesson

Try using the following formats for the Morning Message. As the school year goes on, you can vary the phrases, but the basic format of an introduction, body, and closing should remain constant. Use these terms as you compose the greeting, saying something like, "Let's work on the introduction first," "What can we say in the body today?" or "Now, how can we write a strong closing?"

PREPARATION:
None.

TIME ALLOTTED:
20 to 30 minutes depending on students' ability level.

MATERIALS:
Chart paper and markers.

Paragraph 1, Introduction

Today is _____. The season is _____. The weather this morning is _____ and _____. ←

Begin with one descriptor, and gradually add two or more weather words. Later in the year, add an extension sentence (e.g., "We all had to wear heavy coats today") and an exclamatory word (e.g., "Burrr!").

Paragraph 2, Body

Today we will... ←

In the earliest days of kindergarten, this may be only one sentence, but gradually this should become two or three sentences about special-area classes (art, music, PE, computer), fun activities (playing with clay, painting, watching a movie, going to the playground) or completing a unit or holiday craft or project.

Paragraph 3, Body

It is an important day because... ←

This can be any reason: "It is two days until Spring Break!"; "It is Joey's birthday!"; "Our hamster is about to have babies"; "We're going to use clay"; or "We're going to the zoo!" Once again, it can start out with one sentence, and during the course of several months grow to two or three.

Paragraph 4, Closing

We think today will be _____! ←

Try to elicit a variety of adverbs or adjectives to fill this space. Students will often suggest simply "good" or "fun," and you should use such words frequently so that they will learn to recognize them. But students generally tire of them over time and will try for more exciting endings. How about: "We think today will be...terrific, wonderful, exciting, long, short, hot, wet, snowy, messy, scary (at Halloween), dirty (if you are going to the playground), musical, artistic, delicious, and so on. Eventually, see if students can compose a phrase instead of using just one word to describe the day—for example, "We think today will be messy, but fun."

Sample

Today is Friday. The season is fall. The weather this morning is cool and sunny. The sky is very, very blue.

Today we will have music class. We will play instruments.

It is an important day, because we will go to an assembly. Some people will present a puppet show. We think it will be a funny show.

We think today will be wonderful!

Our Fall Day
Today is   The season
is   The weather is

Today we will

Today is important because

We think today will be

This chart shows the basic format for a Good Morning Greeting.

Today is Friday. The season is fall. The weather this morning is cool and sunny.

Today we will have music class

It is an important day because we will go to an assembly.

We think today will be wonderful!

This chart shows a completed Good Morning Greeting with five topic sentences.

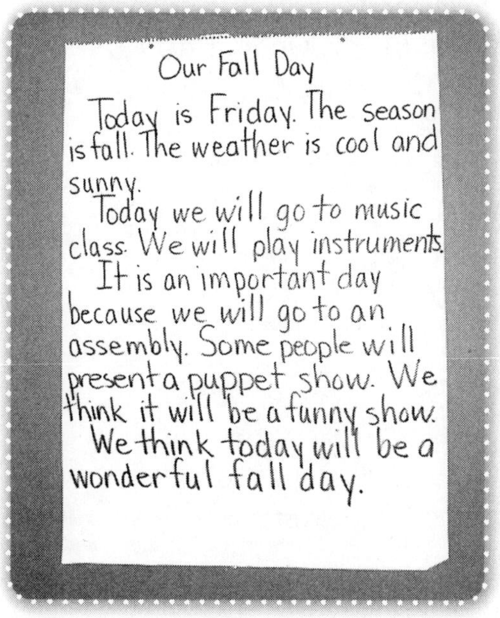

Our Fall Day
Today is Friday. The season is fall. The weather is cool and sunny.
Today we will go to music class. We will play instruments.
It is an important day because we will go to an assembly. Some people will present a puppet show. We think it will be a funny show.
We think today will be a wonderful fall day.

This chart shows the same Good Morning Greeting with topic sentences and extensions added for support. Notice that the story has a title and is "written in a circle." (The word "fall" is found in both the title and the closing.)

Alternate Format

It's _____! ←

> day of week, holiday, someone's birthday, special school event day

It is a good day to _____ and _____. ←

> verbs—sing, paint, decorate, play, read

This morning our class can _____.

After lunch we will _____.

We are _____ that today is _____.

> emotion word ↑

Sample

It's Tuesday! It is a good day to read and play.

This morning our class will read about Clifford. We will make our own Cliffords out of red paper.

After lunch we will go outside to the playground. We will ride the bikes and play in the sand.

We are glad that today is a Clifford day!

Name _____ Date _____

It Is a Good Day

Finish the sentences.

It is a good day to

_____ and _____

This morning our class

can _____

After lunch we will _____

We are _____ that

today is _____

15 Easy Lessons That Build Basic Writing Skills in Grades K-2 Scholastic Professional Books

19

See page 19 for a reproducible of this.

Interactive Writing Activities: Invite Students to Come to the Chart

☀ Invite students to use pointers to lead the class in reading the stories out loud.

Tara uses a magic wand as a pointer. As she points to each word, the rest of the class reads the Good Morning Greeting out loud.

☀ Ask students to come up to the Morning Message and find specific names, or capital letters, or number, color, or size words.

Independent Writing Activity: Finish the Sentence

Give the reproducibles on pages 18 and 19 to students who are ready for an independent writing activity based on the Good Morning Greeting. The phrases are the same as the ones you use every day, and students can either copy words from a model greeting or choose their own to finish the sentences. Notice that periods are not included on the reproducible; this will encourage children to write more than one word and to remember to add a period at the end of each sentence.

Name _____   Date _____

Today

Finish the sentences.

Today is _____

The season is _____

The weather this morning

is _____

Today we will _____

_____

It is an important day

because _____

_____

I think today will be _____

_____

It Is a Good Day

Finish the sentences.

It is a good day to

and

This morning our class

can

After lunch we will

We are   that

today is

Choosing a Title

Skill Focus: *Identifying Main Idea*

CONNECTION TO WRITING ASSESSMENTS . . . .

- ❄ Introduces main idea.
- ❄ Introduces alliteration.
- ❄ Builds awareness of rhyme.
- ❄ Models conventions of print.

When writing Good Morning Greetings (or the Afternoon News, discussed in Chapter 3), make sure you give the finished product a title. The process of discussing title possibilities and choosing an appropriate one focuses students on the main idea of the piece. You can even introduce the concept of audience by helping students consider how a title would encourage someone to read the greeting.

Working with titles also lays the groundwork for positive performance on writing assessments. "What would make a good title for this story?" "What is this story about?" "What is the main idea of this piece?" are all samples of test questions found on assessments of intermediate students. Each is a way of asking students if they can identify the main topic of a piece. By adding titles to Good Morning Greetings in the primary grades, children learn the purpose of a title, how to create effective ones, and how to capture the focus of a piece in a few words. Titles for Good Morning Greetings should, naturally, begin very simply: "Our Day at School," "Today Is Wednesday," "Our Zoo Trip," and the like.

Students respond to Good Morning Greetings

Encouraging students to use alliteration and rhyming words when creating titles adds a fun twist. Young children may not even be able to say "alliteration," much less define it, but the appeal of words that start with the same letters and sounds or that rhyme is easy for them to appreciate. Advertisers have taken advantage of this appeal in naming breakfast cereals, candies, and cartoon characters (Cap'n Crunch, Mars Bars, Mickey Mouse). Invite students to create titles for Good Morning Greetings or other classroom stories that capitalize on this language play. My students' titles have included "Patty's Perfect Party," "Wacky Wednesday," "Cool School," and "Lunch Bunch." The skill and variety of students' ideas improves with practice!

Presenting the Lesson

Write the Good Morning Greeting as discussed in Lesson 1. At the end of the writing experience, read the greeting and ask the class to suggest a title. Explain that a title expresses the main idea of a piece of writing and that it should inspire readers to read the piece. At the beginning of the school year, students will come up with plain titles like "It Is Wednesday," "Joey's Birthday," and "Art Class." This is fine. It establishes the idea of a title, and students will become more creative with experience, especially if you introduce alliteration and rhyming.

PREPARATION:
Collect six to eight books that have an alliterative title.

TIME ALLOTTED:
30 minutes.

MATERIALS:
Chart paper and markers.

Once your students are comfortable generating titles, stretch them a little further. After writing a Good Morning Greeting, pause before discussing a title and display a selection of picture books with alliterative titles. Read the titles aloud while showing the covers of the books, and ask students what they notice. Hopefully, someone will recognize that the words start with the same letters and have the same starting sounds. If that does not happen, have the class practice saying the titles and, exaggerate the alliteration in each one; eventually, someone will point it out. (Some alliterative titles include *Moon Mouse, Stone Soup, Black Beauty,* and *Mike Mulligan.*)

After the class recognizes the matching letters and sounds, have them brainstorm alliterative titles for the Good Morning Greeting. Write these on a separate sheet of chart paper or the chalkboard so that they can see the use of the same letters. (Keep this list, referring and adding to it when creating titles on other days.) Make a class decision, and choose a title for the day's Morning Greeting.

Repeat this process with rhyming book titles such as *The Cat in the Hat, Is Your Mama a Llama?* and *There's a Wocket in My Pocket.* Be sure that your students can see which letters match up in the rhyming words.

Sample Message With Alliterative Title

Wonderful Wednesdays

Today is Wednesday. It is Joey's birthday. He is six years old. We will have cupcakes.

We will have pizza for lunch. We have pizza every Wednesday.

We will go to art class today. Mrs. Jones says we can paint. We will wear smocks.

We like Wednesdays.

Sample Message With Rhyming Title

Monday Funday

Today is Monday. It is cold and rainy outside. We will stay in for our playtime.

Our class got a new computer. It is an iMAC. It is pink.

We get a special treat today. We get to make scarecrows out of paper and straw. We think they will be colorful scarecrows. We will hang them up on our door. We will hear a scarecrow story.

Monday is a fun day for us.

Sample Good Morning Message.

Interactive Writing Activity: Easy Rhyme and Alliteration

❄ Choose a word from the greeting, and have students brainstorm words that rhyme with it. Record their suggestions on the side of the chart or a new sheet of chart paper.

❄ Ask students to find words in the message that begin with a specific consonant or consonant blend, and challenge them to brainstorm more words beginning the same way.

Independent Writing Activity: Illustrate the Message

Have students copy just the title and draw a picture to illustrate one thing in the message.

Invite students to say or write one sentence that could have been included the message. Use the word "I" or a child's first name in the sentence. (Example: "I will have peanut butter for my lunch.")

Follow-up Ideas

Be sure to emphasize alliteration and rhyming found in other places. Talk about the names of students in the classroom—are any of them alliterative? Notice when books have alliteration or rhyme in the title, and point that out. Look for examples of alliteration and rhyme in movies, foods, cartoons—anywhere! Rhyme is easy for kids to detect, but it will take many, many exposures to alliteration before students recognize it and are able to use on their own.

Building an Awareness of Punctuation

Skill Focus: *Using End Punctuation*

CONNECTION TO WRITING ASSESSMENTS ....

- ❉ Introduces importance of end punctuation.
- ❉ Reinforces concept of main idea through title selection.
- ❉ Demonstrates use of organizational plan.
- ❉ Models conventions of print.

Many children have difficulty punctuating their writing, and teachers in the upper elementary grades work diligently to help students understand where to put punctuation marks. On state assessments, spelling and mechanics don't technically count in the score, yet the absence of proper punctuation makes reading essays difficult and can distort the meaning of an essay, thus affecting the score.

There is no better place to teach punctuation than in your daily modeling of writing during the Good Morning Greeting or Morning Message. But just adding the periods is not enough; primary students need a concrete way to fully grasp this concept. In the activity below, you'll ask students to read sentences aloud and pause where it sounds natural. At those points, they'll actually walk up to the chart and place large red sticky dots—mini "stop signs"—to mark where they hear the breaks. This is great for reinforcing the use of periods and should be repeated many times during the school year.

> **Tip** Many worksheets contain unfinished sentences followed by blank spaces. Students are asked to complete each sentence with a word from a story, a chart, or their imagination. To give students practice using end punctuation, white-out the period at the end of the line or white-out the line and period altogether. Eliminating this "_____." encourages students to both complete the sentence with more than one word and develop the habit of putting a period at the end of a thought.

Presenting the Lesson

After students have had some experience with Good Morning Greetings or the Morning Message (refer to Lessons 1 and 2), write one entire message without any periods. Students may question this or remind you that you are forgetting something. If so, just smile and say that you are doing something very special that might be fun! When the message is finished, read it out loud without pausing where you naturally would for the periods. Ask students if they noticed a difference in the reading and if they can guess what made it sound different. Invite them to read it out loud with you and discuss any difficulties they had in reading it.

Then ask them to read it with you again and to guess where the writer needs to signal the reader to stop. Use this opportunity to discuss where "stop signs" (periods) should go and why they belong there. Then read the greeting a third time, first asking students to raise their hand each time they can hear their voice stop or pause. (You may need to exaggerate these breaks to help students hear them.) Explain that these are the places where stop signs (the red dots) should be placed so that the story "will sound more like talk." When the class decides where a stop sign (period) should go, invite a student to stick a red dot onto the chart in that place.

This entire process helps children realize that if it doesn't sound right, then it probably is not correct, and encourages them to trust their ears. Of course, they will not internalize the concept of periods after just one session. You will need to repeat the lesson several times and follow it up with activities in which students must apply the concept to their own writing. (See Follow-up ideas on page 26.)

PREPARATION:
Purchase 3/4-inch red sticky dots, known as signal dots, available at office supply stores.

TIME ALLOTTED:
20 minutes, beginning when the Good Morning Greeting has been completed.

MATERIALS:
Chart paper, chalkboard, or white board; markers or chalk; 3/4-inch red sticky dots.

Jack and Brian place dots on a Good Morning Greeting.

Interactive Writing Activity: Recognizing Sentences

Ask students to count the number of periods in a Good Morning Greeting. Then have them count the number of capital letters that follow the periods, highlighting how this works like a pattern. Point out that sentences always begin with a capital letter and end with a period. Finally, invite students to number the sentences, giving them practice at identifying the conventions of print that mark a sentence.

Independent Writing Activity: Paper Stop Signs to Reinforce Periods

✸ Encourage students to use red "stop signs" in their journal writing. Help them tape a small "STOP" sign to the top of their red crayon, and remind them to use that crayon to make periods while writing. They can go back to existing stories and add red periods, too.

Ben used his red crayon with a stop sign on top to put periods on his writing paper.

Follow-up Ideas

Recopy a previous Good Morning Greeting on chart paper, omitting all ending punctuation. Ask students to determine where the periods should go as they listen to you read aloud. Ask them to raise their hands each time they hear a pause. Each time they do, ask a student to place a red sticky dot on the chart paper at that spot. When all the periods have been added, read the completed greeting again, with exaggerated pauses at each "stop sign." Finally, compare the greeting with the original version so students can see that the use of periods is consistent.

Read any story, making exaggerated stops where the periods are, and have students raise their hands each time they hear the pause. Give them red dots each time they correctly identify where a period should go, and see how many the class can get in a five-minute time frame. Students can collect their red dots and use them to decorate their writing portfolios. That way they will serve as a reminder to use periods in their writing.

In addition to the 3/8-inch dots used for this activity, also purchase some 1/4-inch "signal dots." If you expect the child to write a piece with five sentences, tear off a strip of five dots and see if they can place these at the correct places in their own essay. Most students love adding the red "stop signs" to a story or essay they have written. Be prepared to distribute additional dots as students lengthen their writing.

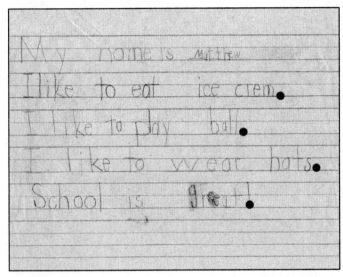

Matthew has used red dots to indicate where periods belong in his essay.

CHAPTER 2

Writing Experience Stories and Other Simple Writing Forms

Now that you've modeled for students the basic structure of a narrative through Good Morning Greetings, it's time to show your young writers how these same elements— introduction, body, closing— play out in other writing forms. In this chapter, I'll share whole-group lessons on writing experience stories, which helps students reflect on important events, and focus on one idea. Next, I'll walk you through lessons on retelling familiar stories. This is a great way to gauge students' comprehension, and an effective way to help students identify and sequence key events, a skill that will serve them well when writing book reports and taking standardized tests. I'll then show you ways to practice using new vocabulary acquired through the day's events, by composing Afternoon News stories. This end-of-day collaboration is a special way to help kids wind down—and reinforce the day's learning. In chapter 3, I'll show you how to guide students to write Afternoon News stories independently.

All these whole-class activities can be done in the context of any content-area topic, and of course allow you to continue to model conventions of print, planning tools, and other writing techniques. The more students can work with an expert writer (you!), the better prepared they'll be to begin writing on their own.

Writing Experience Stories

Skill Focus: *Writing Personal Narratives*

CONNECTION TO WRITING ASSESSMENTS . . . .

- ❈ Introduces personal narrative writing.
- ❈ Introduces use of graphic organizer.
- ❈ Uses action and sound words to liven introduction.
- ❈ Introduces writing in a circle.

The experience story has been a staple of kindergarten writing instruction since the early 1970s. Not to be confused with Good Morning Greetings (class writing about plans for the upcoming day) or the Afternoon News (class writing about the day that is just ending), the experience story is a whole-class think-aloud to record a single event that has recently occurred. And it's come of age: many teachers of grades one, two, three and beyond now write experience stories with their kids. It's most successful when done after something exciting and unusual has happened—someone has visited the class, you've gone on a field trip, carved pumpkins together, or the class hamster has gotten loose.

Presenting the Lesson

In advance of a special activity, invite children to brainstorm words about the upcoming event. For example, a kindergarten class expecting a visit from a rabbit might come up with the following list:

> **PREPARATION:**
> Plan on conducting this lesson after an unusual event. In the following example, we chronicle a rabbit's visit.
>
> **TIME ALLOTTED:**
> About 30 minutes.
>
> **MATERIALS:**
> Chart paper and markers.

Rabbits

soft fur	long ears
eat carrots	hop around

After they visit, when students have experienced a rabbit firsthand and talked about rabbits with an expert, ask them to add to their original list. Their expanded list might look something like this:

Rabbits

soft fur

long ears

eat carrots

hop around

walked, not just hopped

had long toenails

wiggled his nose all the time

washed his face

ate food besides carrots

Next, ask students to take out a sheet of plain white paper, fold it in half, then open the paper and lay it flat on their desks. Tell them to draw what the rabbit looked like on one half and, on the other, to illustrate something the rabbit did. This becomes an elementary graphic organizer they can refer to as the class writes the experience story.

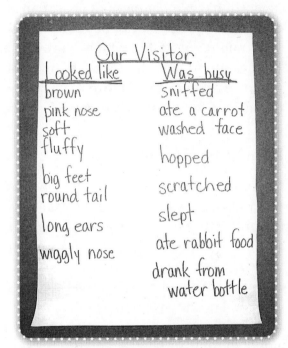

This teacher has created separate columns to indicate that the rabbit's physical description belongs in one paragraph and what the rabbit did in another. This helps students to organize their thoughts before they begin to write.

Logan has drawn pictures of how the bunny looked and how the bunny ate a carrot. Each of these illustrations will become a separate paragraph in the class essay.

Begin with brainstorming: Ask students to offer details about the rabbit's appearance and actions. Encourage them to refer to the rabbit words chart and their illustrations to prompt ideas. Write their suggestions on a big piece of chart paper, leaving a few inches between each sentence so you can better cluster similar details. For example, one child might say, "The rabbit was brown," while the next idea offered is, "The rabbit wiggled his nose." With ample space between these sentences, you can add more physical description and more about the rabbit's movements as children offer them.

Ready to Write!

Once you have written down all details students wish to include, you are ready to begin writing the story. Hang a fresh sheet of chart paper beside the one with the student suggestions. Ask for ideas about how to begin an introduction. Listen to several suggestions and, with the input of your students, write a good introductory sentence or two on the chart. For example, "We had a special treat today. A bunny came to our room."

Now, knowing you want to next address the bunny's appearance, go ahead and choose a topic sentence such as "The bunny was pretty." Talk aloud about your choice, and use the term *topic sentence* so kids begin to hear the language of text structure. Ask, "What should we write about the bunny's appearance?" Write their sentences on chart paper. Then repeat this process for the rabbit's actions, having kids tell you details to add after the topic statement, "The bunny was busy!"

With this lesson, you are teaching the child how to cluster ideas in paragraph form. As soon as you sense kids are ready, have *them* articulate the topic sentences. Lesson by lesson, they come to see that "He ate a carrot" does not belong in the same paragraph as "He has a white tail."

Now, on a fresh sheet of chart paper, write the introduction and copy the story, putting the information into appropriate paragraphs, even if each is only one sentence long.

Then ask for a conclusion to the story. Tell students that an effective way to end a story is writing in a circle: They should choose one word from the introduction and reuse it in the closing. (In the sample, the words *special* and *bunny* are used in both places.) Finally, make sure you have the class add a title to the story, reinforcing the concept of main idea. Ask them to try to make it a special title by using alliteration or rhyming words.

The Funny Bunny

We had a special treat today. A real bunny came to our room.

The bunny was pretty. It was brown. It was pink in its ears. It had a white tail.

The bunny was busy. It hopped around. It wiggled his nose for us. It ate part of a carrot. Then the bunny washed his face.

The visitor was special. His name was "Bugs." He was a funny bunny.

Interactive Writing Activity: Identifying Sensory Words

Ask students to come to the chart paper to identify sensory words in the story—words that describe how something looked, sounded, felt, tasted, or smelled. They can underline each type of sensory detail in a different color, or circle one type, draw a squiggly line under another type, and so on. If any of the senses are not represented, ask students to brainstorm possibilities. Take the opportunity to discuss the importance of choosing sensory details and words that can "paint a picture" for the reader. You might want to give kids a deliberately dull example: "The big elephant was gray" and have them help you make it memorable: "The elephant was slate gray, wrinkled all over his body, and big as a house."

Independent Writing Activity: Adding Details to the Story

Invite students to add a sentence to either body paragraph. For example, In the paragraph about the rabbit's movements, a student might add, "He also scratched behind his ear." To the one about appearance, a student might add, "It's ears hung down." Students might instead wish to add a sentence that uses their names or the first-person pronoun: "Joey got to pet it first," or "I saw him hop really fast."

How do kids make their additions? There are two easy ways: leave spaces on the main chart and allow students to come up and write their own personal sentence; and make copies of the story for each student, leaving spaces at the end of each paragraph.

Follow-up Ideas . . . .

Choral-read your class story and the extended stories students have done. Remember to point to every word on your chart and have them do the same on their papers. This helps students with word recognition, with learning to move from top to bottom and left to right, and with word/sound associations. Pause occasionally and ask students to recite their personal sentences.

Write experience stories throughout the school year. Although the first few times it may be time-consuming, the process will get faster as students tune in to what is valued in a narrative. It will also provide practice for expository writing, as this next example shows.

Sample of Expository Experience Story

Chart Created Before the Pumpkin Carving Experience:

Pumpkin

round	orange	jack-o-lantern
vine	Halloween	pie

Chart Created After Experience

Pumpkin

round	orange	vine	jack-o-lantern
Halloween	pie	slimy	carved
smelly	seeds	strings	face
candle	yellow	glowing	heavy

Notice that the quality of the words is far better after the children have participated in the event. They would not have said "slimy" and "smelly" if they had not touched the pumpkin pulp and smelled it. Quality writing often depends on quality experiences for the child!

Experience Story

Our Plump Pumpkin

We had a pumpkin. First we cut off the top. Then we took out the seeds and strings. Last we carved a face. Our pumpkin looked scary.

Note that this experience story is expository in form, meaning that it focuses on describing a sequenced set of tasks, rather than focusing on a story about the pumpkin-carving. Most primary-grade stories are narrative, so this provides experience with a new type of writing.

Revision

Here is our experience story, with descriptive words, extensions and an exclamation added.

Our Plump Pumpkin

We had a big orange pumpkin. First we cut off the top. It was round. Then we took out the seeds and string. So messy! Last we carved a face. We gave it a mean mouth. Our pumpkin looked scary. Boo!

Editing Written Work

Skill Focus: *Editing to Improve Writing*

CONNECTION TO WRITING ASSESSMENTS ....

❄ Demonstrates how to improve writing by adding extensions.

❄ Models use of strong vocabulary.

Teachers of the primary grades accept—even celebrate—almost anything a child writes. Writing is so complex that we routinely overlook poor spelling, the lack of print conventions, and grammatical errors as a child learns the basics of forming letters and words. And this is as it should be, for the last thing a beginning writer needs is criticism about their independent writing. But this doesn't mean these kids are too young to learn that the meaning of their message can be enhanced by simple revision. If you keep the editing emphasis on clarifying meaning instead of correcting errors, I promise you'll delight rather than discourage your young writers.

In this lesson, you'll learn how to *model* revision and editing techniques during shared writing to help students realize that the best ideas are often afterthoughts and that with a little work and an eraser, their writing can be greatly improved.

The most basic editing appropriate for prewriters involves only three parts: using a caret(^) to insert or replace a word, adding sound words or exclamatory phrases, and adding whole sentences to enhance meaning. You can model these techniques using Good Morning Messages, experience stories, the Afternoon News, or other stories with which students are familiar (see Lesson 7 on page 44).

Later, as students begin to write independently, you can encourage them to use these techniques to edit their own completed pieces. Like any other skill that is consistently repeated within the same format, children will soon come to accept editing as a natural part of writing and will be proud of the improvements they can make to their own work.

> **Tip** In this lesson, I use the terms edit and revise interchangeably. Use whichever word seems most accessible to your students. Some teachers like to say we revise to clarify meaning, and edit to correct punctuation, spelling, etc. It's your call! The important thing is to keep the tasks for improving a piece very simple.

Presenting the Lesson

Display the text, read it, and discuss the events it describes. Use a marker to underline any noun, and ask students if they can think of a word you could add to better describe that person, place, or thing. Encourage them to come up with a variety of descriptors, ranging from size to smell to taste to texture to age, and so on. Then pick one or two that enhance the text and insert a caret and the chosen words.

You'll need to nudge students to get beyond ho-hum answers. For example, If a sentence from a chart reads "We like to eat ice cream," prompt kids to elaborate beyond the obvious chocolate, strawberry, vanilla, and so on. Get them to think in terms of descriptive *phrases*. For example, remind them that ice cream has other qualities besides taste—it can be hard or soft, melted, homemade, crunchy, even Baskin-Robbins. Tell them they can even put the descriptive word after the topic, e.g., "We like to eat ice cream *sandwiches*."

After you have added a few words to the text, then model how to insert one appropriate exclamation word. (Model use of just one really expressive word, or your students will want to fill pages with only these fun words!) The exclamation word can go anywhere in the story, and can be a sound word, (*ding, dong, wham, tweet*) an expression (*wow!, super!, OK!, boo!*) or an action word (*giggle, snicker, pant, blink*).

Adding an Extension

Now, invite children to come up with another sentence to explain or enhance the existing text. You might call it a "detail sentence." For example, if a Good Morning Message contained the sentences, "We like to eat ice cream. We have it for lunch on Tuesdays," an appropriate extension would be: "We eat our ice cream with a wooden spoon," or "Sometimes our ice cream is orange sherbet."

CAUTION: You may not want to perform all three steps the first time you demonstrate revising. Instead, focus on one thing at a time until your students are comfortable with it, and then introduce another. As always, take your cues from your students.

Interactive Writing Activities: Wow Charts and Color Word Displays

❈ Divide students into pairs, and give each pair a large index card. Ask them to brainstorm a variety of exclamations—*POW! BAM! Crunch! Zip! Wiggle!*—and to attempt to spell them. Display the suggestions on a "WOW!" bulletin board. Encourage students to use these to spice up future writing. (You may have to establish a limit of one or two per piece!) Have students be on the lookout for new words for the chart when reading books and cartoons.

❈ Make a large rainbow on a bulletin board, with the largest arc red, followed by orange, yellow, green, blue, indigo, and violet. Give students sticky notes to record how many color words they can think of, writing one word on each sheet. Then put each sticky note onto the appropriate arc of the rainbow; e.g., on the red arc, put sticky notes for *rose, raspberry, scarlet, pink, crimson.* When searching for more precise, lively color words while writing, students can refer to this rainbow

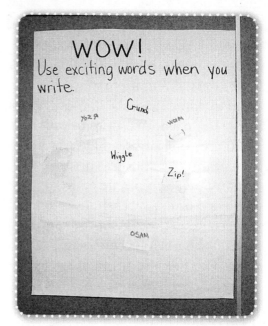

Students have used invented spelling to add words to this "Excitement Chart."

Independent Writing Activity: Adding for Meaning

Copy an old Good Morning Greeting or other shared-writing text onto regular paper, and reproduce it for the class. Be sure to skip lines so children have space to write and make improvements. Encourage them to use the charts in the room, other Good Morning Greetings, or their own imaginations to add an exclamation word, a caret with a describing word or phrase, or even an independent sentence.

Follow-up Idea . . . .

Now that kids have a sense of descriptive words (often adjectives), show them the benefits of using specific nouns and vivid verbs. Show them why *rose* is more specific than *flower* and why *skipped* is more lively than *went.* Ask them to find bland nouns and verbs and replace them with more exciting ones. Then compare the old text with the new text to demonstrate how their writing has really come alive.

LESSON 6

Embellished Retellings of Familiar Stories

Skill Focus: *Sequencing Events*

CONNECTION TO WRITING ASSESSMENTS

* Provides practice in sequencing events.
* Helps students identify key events and differentiate them from nonessential details.

Class discussions that follow a read-aloud are imbued with the magic of the story—and also rich with teachable moments. Through these conversations, you can gauge students' comprehension, build their vocabulary, help them make personal connections to texts, and encourage them to recall key events. In this lesson, I'll share how I extend the discussion by inviting students to help me retell the story in writing.

This exercise serves several purposes. Students get another opportunity to observe an expert writer at work as you model writing your thoughts. It also helps students to focus on the sequence of events and determine the main idea of a story. You can encourage them to provide relevant supporting details and use appropriate describing words. You can also demonstrate writing techniques such as writing in a circle. The more experience students have with these elements, the better prepared they'll be for future writing challenges.

When choosing stories for this activity, try to include fiction stories to complement the nonfiction units you may be teaching. For the insect unit? Be sure to read *The Very Hungry Caterpillar* by Eric Carle. Transportation? Don't forget *Mike Mulligan And His Steam Shovel* by Virginia Lee Burton. Community Helpers? Try *Make Way for Ducklings* by Robert McCloskey. The following example features Beatrix Potter's *The Tale of Peter Rabbit*, which the kids and I read around the time of the bunny's visit, and is part of a Woodland Animals unit.

Presenting the Lesson

After reading a story aloud to your class and discussing it, invite students to help you retell it in writing. Begin by asking them to brainstorm what they remember. As they suggest events, write them on chart paper, placing them in order of their occurrence, and leaving space to add more as they're recalled. For instance, with *Peter Rabbit*, students first reported that the mother was going shopping, which was the beginning of the story. Then they recalled that Peter's sisters went out to pick berries. Knowing that they had skipped some events they would likely recall later, I left a space above the sentence about berry-picking. Eventually, the students did recall the mother's warning and that Peter had on new clothes—both of which occurred before the berry-picking—and those incidents were inserted.

After the brainstorming and recording, ask the class to select three or four events they think are the most significant—events that would help someone who hasn't read the story understand what happens in it. Circle or underline these main events, which will become topic sentences in the retelling. (The balance can be included as extensions, as supporting details, or can be left out.)

In the following retelling of *Peter Rabbit*, the highlighted sentences are those the students selected as the main events. (The numbers indicate the order the sentences were suggested by the class; they would not be listed on the student chart.)

PREPARATION:
Read a story out loud to the class. For best results, the story should relate to an ongoing unit of study, a holiday, or a class project.

TIME ALLOTTED:
About 30 minutes, not including the story time.

MATERIALS:
Chart paper, markers, and the book you have just read.

Tip This method—recording events and leaving space to fill in missing ones—is far more effective than listing everything that happened as students recall it and then numbering them all. Our youngest children have just-developing concepts of numbering, so a list of random events accompanied by numbers would have little meaning for them.

Peter Rabbit

1. Mother rabbit was going shopping.

3. She told the bunnies to pick berries and not to go to Mr. McGregor's garden.

8. Peter had on new clothes.

2. Flopsy, Mopsy, and Cottontail went to pick berries.

4. Peter went to Mr. McGregor's garden.

11. Peter ate lettuce and got sick.

5. Mr. McGregor tried to put a pot on Peter.

6. Mr. McGregor chased Peter with a rake.

7. Peter saw Mr. McGregor's cat.

10. Peter lost his coat and shoes in the garden.

9. Peter ran back under the fence.

12. Flopsy, Mopsy, Cottontail, and Mother had berries and milk.

13. Peter had to drink tea and go to bed.

14. Peter was in trouble for losing his new clothes.

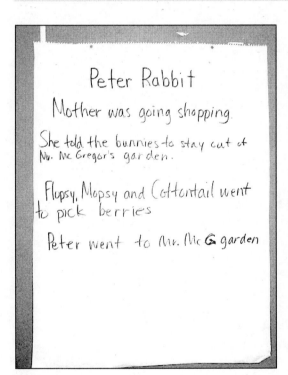

These two charts show the progression of student responses. Notice that there was a space left between sentences so the teacher could continue to add information suggested by the children.

Now, for the embellishment of the retelling: After you've underlined your class's choices of key events, ask them to compose an introduction. Emphasize that this is not a retelling of the story's own beginning, but rather their chance to introduce their feelings about the story, and to entice someone to read the story. (See the three-sentence *Peter Rabbit* introduction below.)

Next ask students to help you turn the highlighted sentences into the body of the retelling. Each key event must be included, and supporting detail can be added. Finally, work together to write an ending, reminding students not merely to recap how the story ended but also to express their feelings about the story.

Embellished Retelling of Familiar Story

Peter Rabbit

We read about Peter Rabbit. He was a naughty bunny. He did not listen to his mother.

introduction

Peter's sisters picked berries for supper. Peter did not help. He went to Mr. McGregor's garden. Mr. McGregor tried to catch Peter, but he got away. He lost his coat and shoes and didn't get any berries and milk.

body

Peter was a really naughty rabbit. He didn't listen to his mother. We hope he learned his lesson!

closing

Interactive Writing Activities: ReRead and Find

❁ Ask students to find all of the characters' names and to notice the capital letter(s) beginning each one.

❁ Have students identify the part that describes the actual story (the body [second paragraph]) and the parts that are enbellished by the class (the introduction [first paragraph] and closing or conclusion [last paragraph].)

❁ Invite students find all of the words that represent Peter Rabbit (*Peter, he, bunny, rabbit*) to start a discussion of pronouns, synonyms, and varied word choice.

Independent Writing Activity: Story Extension

When Peter came home to his mother, he had to tell her what happened to his clothes. Ask students to write what they think Peter might have said to her to explain the disappearance of his shoes and coat. You may want to underline clothing words on the chart to help kids with conventional spelling.

Writing activities such as this can be assigned with almost any story. Remember to ask the child to write an extension about only a small portion of the story. In this case, we did not ask them to tell mother what happened that day, just what happened to his clothes. By limiting the scope of the questions, you give the child more direction and help to assure success.

Composing the Afternoon News

Skill Focus: *Writing With Voice*

CONNECTION TO WRITING ASSESSMENTS . . . .

- ❉ Demonstrates voice in writing.
- ❉ Provides practice in sequencing events.
- ❉ Helps students identify key events and differentiate them from nonessential details.
- ❉ Models personal narrative writing.

Many teachers elect to write the Afternoon News at the close of the day, either in place of or in addition to a Good Morning Greeting. While the Afternoon News covers some of the same territory, instead of looking forward to events, it is more reflective, asking students to report not only what happened that day but also how they felt about it. In fact, there are several advantages to writing Afternoon News versus Good Morning Greetings:

Benefits of Writing Afternoon News Stories ❉

- ❉ **Children are often eager to participate in writing the Afternoon News.** Because they have actually experienced the events being chronicled, it's easier for them to respond more personally and specifically. Shy children, especially, have an easier time with the Afternoon News than with Good Morning Greetings. To further draw them out, prompt them with questions about the activities, stories, and conversations they experienced that day.

- ❉ **The Afternoon News is often about tangible items.** If students created something—e.g., a clay animal, a vocabulary-words chart, a holiday ornament—it is now, of course, right in front of them. That makes it easier for kids to come up with descriptions (size, shape, smell, color content), which improve the quality of the writing.

- ❉ **Students have the opportunity to use vocabulary words acquired that day.** For example, if you were doing a study of Johnny Appleseed and made applesauce together, the children might use words such as peel, core, seed, mash, cinnamon, hot, steamy, and delicious. A chart of relevant vocabulary learned during an activity makes a wonderful resource for the Afternoon News.

❋ **Students are likely to have opinions of what they enjoyed or disliked, which adds emotion or voice.** Voice is one of the toughest qualities of writing to teach; the voice that emanates from a strong opinion often captures the "naturalness" we admire in writing that is said to have voice.

Early-in-the-Year Ease-ins to the Afternoon News

To prepare students for writing the Afternoon News, gather them on the carpet at the end of the day. Discuss everything that happened. Refer to the Good Morning Greeting to see if the day went as planned or if something was changed or left out. (If you wish, insert sentences into the Good Morning Greeting to make it more complete and to model editing techniques.)

Early in the year, this may be all you do; just clarify and correct the Good Morning Greeting. Later in the year, as students become more used to coming to school and to attending to academic work longer, you might want to extend the end-of-day discussion into the Afternoon News and eliminate the Good Morning Greeting altogether. You can replace the greeting with a simple list of events scheduled for the day. Most teachers agree that Good Morning Greetings provide a comfortable beginning for early writers, but as their skills develop, they enjoy the excitement of Afternoon News.

Presenting the Lesson

Reread and discuss the Good Morning Greeting. Then start a new chart called Afternoon News. Ask students to brainstorm memorable things that happened during the day, leaving space after each main event so children can later give you supporting details.

PREPARATION:
None.

TIME ALLOTTED:
Begin with 10 or 15 minutes, and gradually move up to about 30.

MATERIALS:
Chart paper and markers; paper and pencils for students.

Tip Don't expect children to retell the day's activities in order of occurrence. If you ask, "Who can tell me something they remember about today?" instead of "Who can tell me what we did first today at school?" then virtually every child can participate.

Now start on a fresh page, keeping the brainstormed list displayed. Read over that list, and ask students to help you write an introduction. Explain that it should not be an event that happened but rather should express students' feelings about the day. They might suggest, "Today was a super day in our classroom," "Today was the best day of the year," or "Something very sad happened in our class today." Encouraging students to describe their feelings in print helps them bring voice to writing.

Next, turn to the body of the news, reminding students they may refer to both the brainstormed list and the Good Morning Greeting. They should help you create at least two paragraphs of clustered information describing the day's important events. In other words, each paragraph should contain information on the same topic. (As always, leave sufficient space for additional comments.)

Then, end the Afternoon News with a paragraph that, like the introduction, is a summing up of the students' view of their day. You might remind children to write in a circle—reflecting on something that was in the introduction—and to use emotion words to give voice to the writing. ("We will always remember how much fun we had today." "We are sorry that this is Joey's last day." "We loved learning about Christopher Columbus.")

Last, devise a title to the Afternoon News. Ask for class suggestions that might be alliterative, rhyming, or just clever, catchy phrases.

The Great Grade

This was a great day to be in the first grade.

Our class got to go to art. We finger painted using chocolate pudding. It was great. Everyone licked their hands for a treat.

After art class, we heard a story about a boy who found goggles. Big boys tried to take them away. It was an exciting story. It was called *Goggles* by Ezra Jack Keats.

When it was lunchtime, we ate in our classroom. We like that because the cafeteria is SOOOOO noisy.

Now we are sorry to leave school. We all had a great day today.

Notice all the elements of good writing in the above sample: A title;

writing in a circle (use of the word *great* in the introduction and closing); transition words (*when* and *now*) to begin paragraphs; topic sentences followed by extensions; descriptive words; underlining for a story title; proper conventions of print; and an alliterative title.

Interactive Writing Activity: Eliminate Repetition with Revision

In "The Great Grade" sample, *great* appears four times, including the title. Ask students for alternatives to this word. Then, have them come up with more vivid vocabulary for any words they find are uninteresting. Use sticky notes to cover each occurrence of the word, and see what replacements students can come up with. Practice reading the story and substituting alternate words, (Encourage students to aim for specific nouns and vivid verbs.)

Independent Writing Activity: Elaborate

After writing Afternoon News together a few times, suggest that students copy at least one paragraph from the class story chart and add one or two sentences of their own. In "The Great Grade" example, a child might add, "I even had pudding on my nose." See if the student can place the sentence in the appropriate place, thus indicating that she is beginning to understand paragraphing.

CHAPTER 3

Beginning Independent Writing

When a child is in the "scribbling stage" of writing, every person who looks at her work is likely to read it a different way. None of the responses may reflect what the child was actually thinking when she wrote the piece.

Later in their development, children are often amazed that no matter who is reading a familiar story to them, while the voice may vary, the words remain the same. This realization is vital to furthering the child's writing development.

One of the first things a bona fide beginning writer will do is hand a paper to any adult in sight and declare, "Read this!" Imagine the Aha! moment the child experiences when she realizes that no matter whom she shows her writing to, they all read it the same way!

Writing is one of the most difficult skills we ever expect children to learn. Providing them with a format to get them started is really just a kindness, much like holding onto their hands when they first learn to walk. A simple, familiar format allows a child to feel successful, because others can read what he has written.

The lessons in this chapter provide the structured handholding new writers need. They build on the skills you've introduced in previous lessons, and give students the tools they need to become independent writers. As soon as students are comfortable with these formats, they are ready for more freedom and can move on to the lessons in Chapter 4.

Child-Written Afternoon News

Skill Focus: *Word Choice*

CONNECTION TO WRITING ASSESSMENTS . . . .

❋ Demonstrates using a graphic organizer to plan writing.

❋ Models including voice in an essay.

❋ Helps students choose words carefully.

. . . .

After students have had practice creating the Afternoon News as a class, they are ready for some independent writing. Do not, however, expect that you can distribute the reproducible pages (pages 54–56) and get a good result. Most of your students are probably not yet ready for that level of independence. Instead, the first two or three times you do this activity, do it as a whole group, encouraging every student to "stay with you" as you gently guide them through how to write their own Afternoon News.

The reproducibles in this book have a space for illustrations and formatted text to guide students toward independent writing. If students desire more room for illustrations, give them a blank sheet of paper or have them illustrate the other side of the reproducible. The illustrations are a primitive graphic organizer—they give students a jumping-off point for their writing—and the familiar text gives them confidence that they can complete the assignment. A large writing space encourages them to use more than one word, and the exclusion of periods gives them practice with ending punctuation periods. At least one sentence requires students to begin it, so they get practice in capitalization. And since the sentences are triple-spaced, students can practice the editing skills you've modeled, using carets to insert words.

Presenting the Lesson

Distribute copies of the reproducible on page 54, and allow time for students to write their names and to copy the name of the day as you model writing it on the chart.

PREPARATION:

1. Copy the reproducible on page 54, making about five extra for students who "mess up."

2. Copy the text onto chart paper exactly as it appears on the reproducible.

3. Display relevant Good Morning Greetings, Afternoon News, experience stories, or other word charts.

TIME ALLOTTED:
30 to 45 minutes.

MATERIALS:
Copies of the reproducibles on page 54; chart paper and markers; previous Good Morning Greetings, Afternoon News, experience stories, or other relevant word charts.

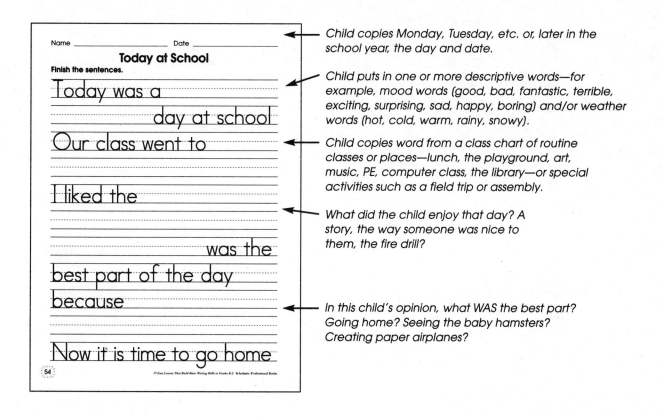

Child copies Monday, Tuesday, etc. or, later in the school year, the day and date.

Child puts in one or more descriptive words—for example, mood words (good, bad, fantastic, terrible, exciting, surprising, sad, happy, boring) and/or weather words (hot, cold, warm, rainy, snowy).

Child copies word from a class chart of routine classes or places—lunch, the playground, art, music, PE, computer class, the library—or special activities such as a field trip or assembly.

What did the child enjoy that day? A story, the way someone was nice to them, the fire drill?

In this child's opinion, what WAS the best part? Going home? Seeing the baby hamsters? Creating paper airplanes?

Name _____ **Date** _____

Today at School

Finish the sentences.

Today was a

         day at school

Our class went to

I liked the

         was the

best part of the day

because

Now it is time to go home

54

15 Easy Lessons That Build Basic Writing Skills in Grades K-2 Scholastic Professional Books

---

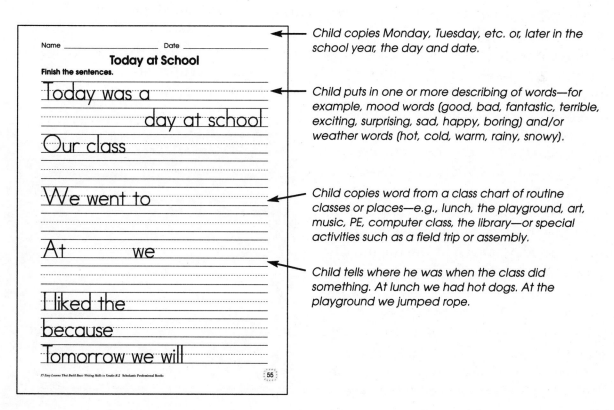

Child copies Monday, Tuesday, etc. or, later in the school year, the day and date.

Child puts in one or more describing of words—for example, mood words (good, bad, fantastic, terrible, exciting, surprising, sad, happy, boring) and/or weather words (hot, cold, warm, rainy, snowy).

Child copies word from a class chart of routine classes or places—e.g., lunch, the playground, art, music, PE, computer class, the library—or special activities such as a field trip or assembly.

Child tells where he was when the class did something. At lunch we had hot dogs. At the playground we jumped rope.

Name _____ **Date** _____

Today at School

Finish the sentences.

Today was a

         day at school

Our class

We went to

At   we

I liked the

because

Tomorrow we will

55

15 Easy Lessons That Build Basic Writing Skills in Grades K-2 Scholastic Professional Books

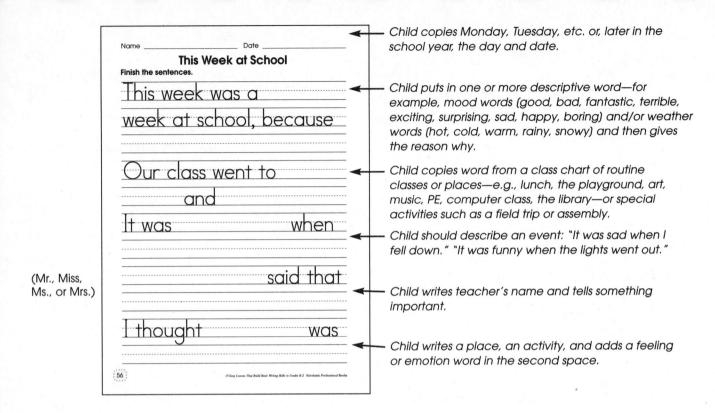

Child copies Monday, Tuesday, etc. or, later in the school year, the day and date.

Child puts in one or more descriptive word—for example, mood words (good, bad, fantastic, terrible, exciting, surprising, sad, happy, boring) and/or weather words (hot, cold, warm, rainy, snowy) and then gives the reason why.

Child copies word from a class chart of routine classes or places—e.g., lunch, the playground, art, music, PE, computer class, the library—or special activities such as a field trip or assembly.

Child should describe an event: "It was sad when I fell down." "It was funny when the lights went out."

Child writes teacher's name and tells something important.

Child writes a place, an activity, and adds a feeling or emotion word in the second space.

Prompt students to draw pictures of at least two things that they wish to write about. (For example, they could illustrate where the class went that day—the playground, the library, PE class, or art class—and something that they enjoyed about it.)

As a class, read the first sentence of the reproducible aloud. Ask students to suggest words that could go in the blank space. As they talk, list the words on a separate sheet of chart paper or the chalkboard.

Ask the class to help you select one word for your model, and write it in the blank space. Together, reread the sentence out loud. Now ask the children to choose one word for their own papers. Those in the earliest stages of writing may copy your word exactly, while more confident writers may select another word from the list. The most advanced will choose a word from their own experience, and may even write more than one word in the space. (Encourage these students to use invented spelling.)

Offer praise to everyone for completing the sentence, regardless of his skill level. Once students have had time to write the word, ask for volunteers to read their

Jack works hard to complete his independent work.

opening sentence to the rest of the class. Providing a variety of words and encouraging students to select their own attunes them to the choices they have as writers and the ways specific words can express their voices.

Repeat the process for the second space, creating a new list of word choices for it. Once again, let the children help you select a word for your model, read the sentence out loud together, then ask them to write a word in their own spaces. Continue in the same way to help students to complete the remaining spaces.

Follow-up Ideas

Moving children toward independent writing isn't a quick and easy process. It will take more than one day for students complete the essays the first few times you do it, but rest-assured, it does get easier. Make sure you save your "suggested words" lists so that you can just add to them each time you repeat the process. Keep using these reproducibles until students are capable of completing them with very little help from you. And always encourage students to write their own extension sentences or add describing words, if they are capable. Supporting details can follow any of the topic sentences that are presented on the reproducibles.

These newsletters can be sent home or kept in a portfolio (pocket manila folders are best as they eliminate many spills). Send them home once a month, share them at parent conferences, refer to them when you are writing your report cards, start new journals or diaries after each reporting period, or save them for the entire year in a portfolio.

Variation

These writing lessons do not have to be completed on the reproducible. Though more time-consuming, there is a great benefit to having students do *all* the writing themselves. Students can practice correct letter formation, paragraphing and spelling if they are copying the basic format without having to think about the words they are adding. If you opt for that, have students make illustrations first, and then pass out paper for them to begin the writing process. Because this is a lot of work for the youngest students, consider writing just one weekly Afternoon News instead of one each day.

Following are three formats (reproducibles) to help children get started independently writing the Afternoon News. Note that they vary greatly in difficulty and in the amount of writing expected.

Today at School

Finish the sentences.

Today was a

        day at school

Our class went to

I liked the

        was the

best part of the day

because

Now it is time to go home

15 Easy Lessons That Build Basic Writing Skills in Grades K-2 Scholastic Professional Books

Today at School

Finish the sentences.

Today was a

day at school

Our class

We went to

At   we

I liked the

because

Tomorrow we will

Name _____   Date _____

This Week at School

Finish the sentences.

This week was a

week at school, because

Our class went to

and

It was   when

said that

I thought   was

15 Easy Lessons That Build Basic Writing Skills in Grades K-2 Scholastic Professional Books

LESSON 9

Five-Sentence Essays for Early Writers

Skill Focus: *Using a Graphic Organizer as a Planning Tool*

CONNECTION TO WRITING ASSESSMENTS

- ✳ Introduces writing on an assigned topic.
- ✳ Introduces use of graphic organizer as planning tool.
- ✳ Reinforces idea that an essay has an introduction, body, and closing.
- ✳ Encourages the use of voice.
- ✳ Encourages revision and editing of existing work.

This essay writing lesson helps students organize their writing. The first time you present it, plan on it taking about 30 minutes. It will get easier and faster for both you and your students. Meanwhile, the children gain confidence and get excited about extending their writing.

The trick, however, is not to go *too* fast. Whether the project takes two days or up to a week, you'll probably want to assess your instruction. Was the assignment too hard? (typically, it is manageable in the first month of first grade), or were you being exceptionally thorough, for instance allowing every child to share her work? Sometimes a learning experience just takes time! If it is going smoothly and you can see that the children are making progress, don't worry how long it takes before you staple their essays onto the bulletin board.

As in some previous lessons, this activity begins by having children illustrate their essay before they begin to write. Ask them to fold a sheet of paper into quarters and to draw their story in steps. This page becomes a graphic organizer, a valuable planning tool. Because this organizer uses only illustrations and not words, I like to call it a "graphic" graphic organizer!

PREPARATION:
Display previously made charts of favorite games, toys, foods, clothing, and so on. If you do not have these on hand, this lesson will take a while longer but you can still do it; have lots of chart paper on hand to create new charts alongside your writing lesson.

TIME ALLOTTED:
Varies greatly according to children's age and ability. The example(s) here required three 30-minute writing sessions, including the illustrations but not including students reading their stories to the class.

MATERIALS:
Writing and drawing paper and crayons or colored pencils for students; lined chart paper and markers, or chalkboard and chalk, for you.

Presenting the Lesson

DAY ONE: CREATING THE "GRAPHIC" GRAPHIC ORGANIZER

Plan on using the first day simply to complete the graphic organizer. Give each child a sheet of drawing paper and show how to fold it in quarters, then open it and lay it out (see illustration). Next, ask the children to number the four sections of the paper. Demonstrate this on your chart paper or chalkboard, labeling the upper left-hand corner "1," the upper right-hand corner "2," the lower left-hand corner "3," and the lower right-hand corner "4."

In section 1 (upper left), have the students draw self-portraits; in section 2, their favorite foods; in 3, their favorite games; and in 4, their favorite article of clothing. When the illustrations are done, collect the papers and save them for the next part of the lesson.

Cliff has illustrated the things he intends to write about.

DAY TWO: DRAFTING THE STORY

To continue the lesson, hand out grade-level lined writing paper and the illustrations from the previous day. Then walk students through the following steps:

1. Using lined chart paper or the chalkboard, demonstrate where and how students should write a capital M on their papers to begin the essay (see sample on page 59). Note that this "M" should be indented though it is not on the student sample. Check to see if

everyone has started in the appropriate place and written a capital M. Next to the "M," write a lowercase "y," and ask students to do the same. Ask if anyone knows what word she has just written.

2. Leave a space and model how to write the words *name* and *is*, asking students to follow along. Check again to see if they are keeping pace with you. Then ask them to write their name after *is*. (Let it be their choice whether or not to include a last name.) Now, read this sentence aloud together.

3. Next, model where and how to write a capital I to begin a new sentence. (Do not start a new paragraph, even though you'll see that on the model. Children should not get in the habit of starting a new line with each new sentence.) After a quick check around the room, follow that with the words *like* and *to*. Check again and assist any students who are having difficulty. Then go back to the chart and write the word *eat*. Discuss what the sentence says so far, and read the sentence together as a class.

4. Ask the class to look at their illustrations—their "graphic" graphic organizers—to see what their favorite food is. Students can use invented spelling to write the appropriate word at the end of the sentence, or copy the word from a food chart, or ask you how to spell it. (Using a small pad of sticky notes, you could jot down a word when asked and stick it on a student's desk or add it to your existing chart.)

5. Repeat this process with two more sentences, pausing as needed according to the speed and ability of your class. The next two sentences are: "I like to play ____" and "I like to wear _____." Each time, refer students to their organizers and allow them to use invented spelling, look at an existing chart, or ask you for the correct spelling.

6. Finally, model writing the concluding sentence: "I think school is ____." This allows students to add their voices to the pieces, an element essential to older students' writing (and measured on state assessments). The word completing this sentence should be a feeling or emotion word, or even phrase.

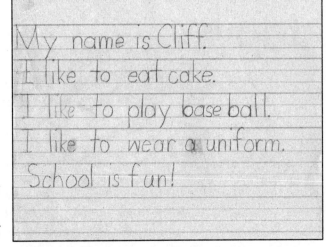

Cliff has written about the items he illustrated in his graphic organizer

7. If you have time, ask several students to read their works to the class and show their illustrations.

8. In some classrooms the writing process will take two days. This is not unusual, especially if you do not have existing charts of words for students to copy.

DAY THREE: EDITING

Returning to your essay chart or the chalkboard, write in your own favorite food, game, and clothing. Read your essay aloud and then ask students for suggestions to improve it. If you "like to eat cashews," ask them what describing words you could add to make the sentence better—big cashews, salty cashews, chocolate-covered cashews! Choose one, make a caret, (^) and add the describing word. Continue in this way through the rest of the model essay.

Twins Lauren and Julie work together to edit a story.

Then ask students to reread their own essays and use carets to add describing words to their essays. If, however, some students are really struggling with this, allow them to solicit suggestions from a peer or students at their table cluster. Remember that another student can suggest a word, but all of the actual writing should be done by the author of the essay. Students should not be allowed to write words on another's paper. On Cliff's sample on page 59, children suggested adding describing words before "cakes"—decorated cakes, chocolate cakes, homemade cakes, and Twinkie cakes.

Follow-up Ideas . . . .

❈ Display the written work and illustrations on a bulletin board titled "All About Us" or "Our First Essays." Save them for growth comparisons throughout the year. Send them home.

❈ Place the essays in a journal.

Variation

In each of the following reproducibles, children are expected to write five-sentence essays using the same steps outlined above, beginning with a "graphic" graphic organizer. These can be presented as reproducibles, or students can do their own writing and copying—the choice is up to you.

Add a title.

I have a friend named

We like to play with

We like to go to

We laugh about

makes me

feel

Name _____ Date _____

_____

- -

_____

Add a title.

We eat lunch at school

I like to eat

I don't like the

                    is my

friend at lunch.

When I eat at school,

I feel

Name _____   Date _____

Add a title.

I like

I like to eat

I like to drink

I like to play

makes me

feel

15 Easy Lessons That Build Basic Writing Skills in Grades K-2 Scholastic Professional Books

Name _____ Date _____

_____

Add a title.

My favorite toy is a

It has

I keep it

I play with it

is a

toy

Writing Field-Trip Reports

Skill Focus: *Developing Main Ideas*

CONNECTION TO WRITING ASSESSMENTS . . . .

- ❄ Choosing key events.
- ❄ Sequencing events.
- ❄ Developing main ideas.

Almost every school tries to provide a few field trips for students in the early grades. Visiting a bakery, the fire station, the post office, a park, a grocery store, a restaurant—these are excellent ways for students to learn about the world beyond their homes and families. They relish discovering the "behind the scenes" activities of familiar places and enjoy the extra attention paid to them by the employees. Though I used to make these trips (and longer ones, by car or bus) as culminations to units about The Zoo, Farm Life, or The Hospital, one day I divined a new twist: We took the field trip first, before we studied the unit!

Preparations for the field trip and the actual trip generate great enthusiasm for the subject *before* it is studied! Children tend to pay far more attention if they are interested in and have a frame of reference for the posters, videos, or stories you are about to present. They return from trips with a wealth of valid questions that can generate in-depth studies of a subject.

If we use the field trip as a culminating activity, the students' enthusiasm peaks just when you return to the classroom and begin a new subject. We often think that children are restless after a trip and will not settle down and "get back to work." In reality, they are full of questions and anxious to learn more, but, eager to keep covering new curriculum, we often redirect their attention to a whole new subject! Think how frustrating it must be to return from a trip to the zoo and the next day start studying about fire safety—just when they most want to know the "why" and "how" about every animal they just saw!

It is difficult to teach students about a subject for which they have very little background knowledge. For example, imagine all the misconceptions a child might have about a giraffe. (A child might think: It is probably as tall as my dad. Its legs are longer than mine. It probably has a mouth like my dog.) Yet, after they have actually stood beside this huge animal and watched it eat and seen the size of its spots, they will be much better able to make sense of the information they will learn during the unit. Obviously, you will still need to introduce the event and provide a little background knowledge before you go. But afterward, you can say, "Remember when we saw the _____?" or "_____" and students will immediately be tuned in to the topic.

As children return from a field trip, consider it a golden opportunity to assess what they learned there and to jump-start some writing practice. In the following example, students are asked to explain in chronological order what they did on their trip. Alternatively, you could invite students to write about their three favorite aspects of the trip or three new things they learned.

Presenting the Lesson

DAY 1

After the field trip, spend a few minutes adding words to the chart you made before you went. These words can be adjectives, nouns, verbs, or even emotion words (giant, cuddle, giraffe, tongue, ran, visited, stared, scared, fascinated, excited).

Each entry should reflect something that the children saw or did or felt while they were on their trip.

Then, on a fresh sheet of chart paper or the chalkboard, together make a chronological list of the three main events (or "favorite parts") of the trip. (Though there will likely be more than three or four, tell students you are going to use only three.)

Pass out only the drawing paper and allow students to draw and discuss the illustrations! (In grades K or 1 you might want to collect these and redistribute them the following day for the writing activity.)

Then pass out writing paper and prepare your chart to use as a model. (Add name and date to the chart as students add their names and the date to their papers.)

This teacher has helped the children list all of the events of their field trip to an Italian restaurant.

PREPARATION:
Return from a field trip. (Remember that these do not have to be major trips. A visit to your school cafeteria kitchen to meet the cooks and see how lunch is prepared can be a learning experience!)

TIME ALLOTTED:
30 to 45 minutes.

MATERIALS:
Writing and drawing paper and crayons or colored pencils for students; lined chart paper and markers, or chalkboard and chalk, for you.

Fazoli's
We got on the bus.
We met the owners of Fazoli's.
We had to go in groups to the kitchen.
We looked at the ovens. We saw the man throw the pizza dough.
We placed our orders. spaghetti fettuchini ziti pizza
We had to wait a long time.
We got to eat lunch.
We got prizes, and leftovers.
We went back to school fast.

Remember that when you are creating the model on the chart paper or chalkboard, go slowly—only one sentence at a time—and keep the majority of the kids "with you" in their writing.

Next, write the following sentence on chart paper or the chalkboard:

Our class went to _____.

Fill in the blank on your model then ask students to copy the sentence on their writing papers. Then add:

First we _____.

Ask students to refer to the chart and to look at their illustrations to help you decide what to write in the space. Choose one for your model, then have students begin copying the sentence. Allow them to either copy your entry, change it slightly, or write in their own "first event." Repeat the process with next two sentences:

Next we _____.

Last we _____.

The closing sentence will begin with the name of the field-trip destination:

_____ was a _____ place to visit.

Last, ask the class to help you add a title.

In the example page below, notice that this teacher had students draw only a small illustration and it is on the same page that the writing appears. This is a great time saver; using this kind of paper keeps the children from wanting to spend such a long time on the illustration.

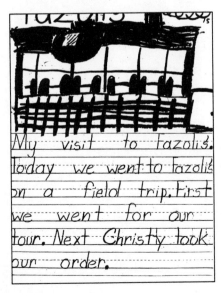

Warning: Don't make the lines indicated in the above sentences, the students will invariably copy those lines on their papers. Ditto for three dots (ellipses) to indicate that the children should continue—they'll just make those three dots wherever you do!

Model Student Essay

Zooooo Zpecial to Us!

Our class went to the zoo. First we visited the reptile house. Next we saw the big cats. Last we looked at the elephants. The zoo was a fascinating place to visit.

Notice the variety of verbs. Inspire the children to be more inventive than "We saw the reptiles. We saw the cats. We saw the elephants" unless it's a kindergarten class or very early in first grade.

DAY 2

If this lesson is being presented late in first grade or in second grade, on the second day, encourage students to revise their work. Since they just went on the field trip, they should have lots of ideas to draw from for adding relevant details or examples to develop their main ideas. Ask them to "say one more thing" about each main idea (more advanced students will write at least two extensions).

Primary writing paper has large spaces between the lines of print, so extra sentences can be added there. Allow the child to complete the five-sentence essay and reread it out loud. The following day, have them look at their work and see if they can think of an additional sentence that would make the story better.

A second way to do this is to have the students cut apart their five-sentence essay. Paste the introduction and first sentence onto a sheet of lined writing paper and then add the extension sentence. Repeat for the third and fourth sentences, and then paste on the closing sentence.

Model Student Essay With Extensions

Yesterday our class went to the zoo. First we visited the reptile house. We saw lots of snakes. Next we saw the big cats. The lion roared a loud roar at us. Last we looked at the elephants. A man was feeding them peanuts. The zoo was a fascinating place for our class to visit. We hope to go again soon.

Summarizing Independent-Reading Books

Skill Focus: *Summarizing Text*

CONNECTION TO WRITING ASSESSMENTS . . . .

* ❈ Choosing key events.
* ❈ Sequencing events.
* ❈ Revising to develop main ideas.

This lesson builds on the skills introduced in Lesson 6: identifying key events, sequencing events, and including an introduction and conclusion. This reinforcement moves students toward summarizing text independently, as they will be required to do for book reports, other academic writing assignments, and standardized tests.

Though designed around a student's independent reading, you can use this activity to follow up a basal reader story or even a video. Keep in mind that it's a challenging assignment that should be repeated several times to give children confidence in their writing skills.

Presenting the Lesson

After modeling how to summarize a familiar story several times, tell students that this time when you read a story they will be asked to do the response writing themselves—but give them a partner and let them work together to do the writing.

First read the book you have chosen out loud and go through the now-familiar process of asking students to tell you events that were in the story. As they retell them to you, record on chart paper, remembering to skip lines so that you can eventually end up with everything in the correct order. Then prompt students to help you to decide what were the three *main* events that happened in the story. Mark them in an appropriate way such as underlining, circling, or highlighting them.

PREPARATION:
Choose a book with a strong main character. (Some suggestions: *Goggles* or *Peter's Chair* by Ezra Jack Keats, *Strega Nona* by Tomie dePaola, *The Cat in the Hat* by Dr. Seuss, *Curious George* by H.A. Rey.)

TIME ALLOTTED:
Two 30-minute writing sessions, one for brainstorming and the second for writing the summary.

MATERIALS:
Writing paper.

Pass out copies of the reproducible on page 72, but this time do not make suggestions to the children about what to write. Instead, let them collaborate with a partner and create an introduction, a body of events from the story, and a closing, using the information on the chart to help them. Because every child is writing about the same book, these may be a little repetitious, so try to encourage students to be creative and to use their very best choice of verbs and adjectives.

Most stories will be only five sentences long, but remember to encourage students to add extensions, thus explaining their topic sentences and adding support to their reports.

Variation

When students become really good at doing this reproducible, suggest that two students read the same book and collaborate on a book report together—without your help in creating a chart. They can use the same reproducible. Remind them that even though it is the same book and they are working together, each report should be slightly different from the other, thus keeping the child's individuality and voice in the piece.

Mason and J.T. work together to write reports about a book they both have read.

Student Sample

We read *Miss Nelson Is Missing* by Harry Allard and James Marshall. In the beginning, the children would not be nice for Miss Nelson. Then Viola Swamp came to be the teacher. At the end, Miss Nelson came back, and the kids were good. We think Miss Nelson was tricky.

Follow-up Ideas

This is a challenging activity for kids the first time around. Try it several times until it becomes easy for your students to complete it by themselves. Eventually, they should be able to not only complete a story summary like the one above, but also to add extension sentences (shown below in italics) to each main event. Notice that each italicized sentence serves to support the topic sentence. Adding these supporting sentences to an essay can raise the score on a fourth-grade assessment as much as an entire point. While they are important for young children and necessary for older ones, try to avoid the temptation of expecting students to do this independently at too young an age. There is plenty of time to do more modeling and give students practice adding elaborations. On the other hand, many students will recognize the value that these add to the essay, and many second graders are ready to include extensions in their work.

Revised Student Sample—with Extensions

We read *Miss Nelson Is Missing* by Harry Allard and James Marshall. In the beginning, the children would not be nice for Miss Nelson. *They acted up during story time.* They threw spitballs. Then Viola Swamp came to be the teacher. *Miss Swamp was mean. She made the children work very hard. They did not have story time.* At the end, Miss Nelson came back, and the kids were good. *They were so glad to see her, they were good all of the time. They even got to have story time again.* We think Miss Nelson was tricky.

Name _____ Date _____

Add a title.

We read

by

In the beginning,

Then

At the end,

We think

15 Easy Lessons That Build Basic Writing Skills in Grades K-2 Scholastic Professional Books

CHAPTER 4

Independent-Writing Activities

When students are comfortable using the structured formats you've introduced and modeled in this book's previous lessons, they are ready to tackle more independent writing. The activities described in this chapter range from journal writing to report writing. They help students to move gradually from adding only a few words to creating an essay complete with elaborations and paragraphs. Because many states ask students to create paragraphs in response to reading passages, there is even a lesson on inferencing and explaining inferences.

If second-grade children can independently use all the skills and strategies presented in this book, they are well on their way to finding great success in most of their school work. They will be in good shape to take performance assessments too. The child who can successfully write in these formats can later move to being more creative, in format, sentence structure, and in paragraph organization. But he can always fall back on these familiar formats for book reports, science and social studies reports, and letter writing.

LESSON 12

Journal Writing

Skill Focus: *Developing Self-expression*

CONNECTION TO WRITING ASSESSMENTS

* Provides independent writing practice.
* Encourages use of sensory details.

As testing pressure mounts, many teachers have abandoned journal writing despite its manifold benefits. What's so wonderful about journal writing? It allows students to express thoughts and ideas about things that matter to them without the pressure of following all the conventions of print. This freedom often fosters a positive attitude toward writing, yet at the same time, students in fact get extra practice in everything from increased skill at the physical act of printing letters, to matching sound and letters together (invented spelling) to organizing their thoughts and sequencing events, to developing voice. From a teacher's point of view, journal entries are excellent for assessing students' needs and planning relevant lessons. (Be sure to read *Fresh Takes on Using Journals to Teach Beginning Writers* by Jim Henry, published by Scholastic, for great ideas on using journals in your classroom.)

Students who have regularly participated in shared writing experiences, such as those described in previous chapters, are often the most successful journal writers because they understand the basics of how to organize and create a piece through observing the consistent modeling of the teacher. If the products of whole-group writing activities— Good Morning Greetings, experience stories, Afternoon News and so on—are displayed along with word walls and subject-matter charts, students will have a great time incorporating these words into their own writing. Students who have been exposed to format writing as part of their writing instruction may even include some of the commonly used phrases in their own work.

Some teachers offer so little guidance during journal time their students make slow progress in written self-expression; others hold the reins so tightly that the finished products are not a personal expression at all. Journal writing in the early grades should be a time to write freely on any subject of the students' choice without worry about getting it all right. The least-skilled writers should be encouraged to illustrate first and then use single words to label their drawing. Eventually this child can move to creating whole sentences to go with the illustration. Timid writers do well if they are allowed to write ON their illustration instead of being faced with that huge blank sheet of white paper.

I recommend encouraging students to illustrate their ideas first; children often express themselves more easily in pictures than in words, so drawing provides inspiration and focus for their writing. For instance, they're more likely to include description if looking at a "large, green tree" or the "long, red fire truck with big, black wheels."

Since children may take several days to complete one story, instruct them to always date their work so that you both can trace their progress as writers. Or buy an inexpensive date stamp, and assign a different child to stamp everyone's paper each day.

Save journal entries by stapling stories with their illustrations and placing them in a "pocket" manila folder (one that has enclosed ends—fewer piles of paper all over the classroom floor!) that has been decorated by the students. They can be a source for lesson plans (helping you identify where students need help), provide a great picture of each student's growth in writing, and offer a glimpse into children's personal lives and intellectual development.

Presenting the Lesson

There are several ways of beginning journal writing, all of which allow children a measure of freedom yet also give them suggestions about what to write (otherwise, they can become frustrated searching for ideas). After trying these a couple of times, you can probably say, "Write about whatever you'd like," and they'll be able to.

Invite students to bring in a stuffed animal or toy and draw it.

PREPARATION:
None.

TIME ALLOTTED:
About 30 minutes two times a week.

MATERIALS:
Writing and drawing paper, pencils, and colored pencils or crayons.

1. In their journals, they can then (a) describe it, (b) tell what it would say if it could talk, (c) write about the day they got it, (d) tell about somewhere they went with it—or (e) all four!

2. Ask children to write their own version of a class experience story.

They can use some of the same words, but encourage them to tell what they saw, how they felt, what they remembered.

3. Have the students (a) draw, then write about, the previous weekend or a past vacation or (b) draw, then write about, what they want to be when they grow up.

4. Make up a story that will make the class laugh.

5. Make up a scary story.

Interactive Writing Activity: Invite Peer Comments

Have students show their illustrations and read their completed journal entries to the class (even if only one or two sentences). Encourage the class to ask questions. The writer may choose to add to the story based on what the other children want to know. Be sure to praise every child who reads aloud, and display the entire class's completed work.

Independent Writing Activity: Finding Details in Pictures

As you circulate around the room during journal-writing time, encourage students to look at the details in their illustrations for inspiration about what to write. Help them choose descriptive words to add by pointing out that they drew a "large green tree" and the "long red fire truck with the big black wheels," or to write details such as, "It was a sunny day." (Most students include a sun in their drawings.) They will eventually learn to rely on their illustrations to get ideas for enhancing their work.

> **Tip** When students ask about spelling, encourage them to use invented spelling or to check classroom spelling resources (the word wall, charts, dictionaries, books). Always carry small sticky notes with you so that if a word is particularly difficult or irregular, you can spell out and leave the sticky note on a child's desk. Suggest that the child copy the word from the sticky note onto the appropriate chart in the classroom. This gives the students real ownership in what is on the walls, provides one more time for him to copy it correctly, and helps him remember where to look if he needs this word again.

Identifying Character Traits

Skill Focus: *Inferring Information About Characters*

CONNECTION TO WRITING ASSESSMENTS . . . .

❈ Making inferences.

❈ Proofreading.

In virtually every state assessment, students score lowest on the parts labeled "inferencing." The ability to read between the lines—to infer information—does not come naturally. For example, if students hear or read a story about a snowball fight at school, they may or may not be able to infer that this story happened in the daytime, not at night; in the winter, as opposed to any other season; that the children would have probably worn mittens or gloves when making their snowballs and that possibly the children involved did not like each other. When faced with inference questions, even fourth and fifth graders will wail, "It doesn't SAY that in the story!"

To build kids' inferencing skills, begin the kinds of activities suggested in this chapter as early as kindergarten. By first grade you can introduce the writing activities suggested below.

Presenting the Lesson

Before reading aloud the selected story, tell students to listen carefully for details about the characters—what the character looks like, what kind of personality he has—because, afterward, you are going to ask for a description. The story discussed in this example is *Strega Nona* by Tomie dePaola.

After reading the story, fold a piece of chart paper in half lengthwise, open it, and write the main character's name at the top. Then label one column "Looks Like" and the other "Personality." As students describe the character, list the physical descriptions, and the traits in the other column.

The latter will require some prompting from you. Young students find this task difficult, because

> **PREPARATION:**
> Choose a book with a strong main character. (Some suggestions: *Mufuro's Beautiful Daughter* by John Steptoe, *Madeline* by Ludwig Bemelmans, *Min Lo Moves the Mountain* by Arnold Lobel, *Sylvester and the Magic Pebble* by William Steig)
>
> **TIME ALLOTTED:**
> Two 30-minute writing sessions.
>
> **MATERIALS:**
> Writing and drawing paper, pencils, and colored pencils or crayons.

usually the traits are not expressly stated in the story; children must infer a person's character traits based on the actions and words of that character. To get the class started, try asking if anyone would like big Anthony for a friend. If a child responds, "no," ask why not. If she says that Big Anthony is careless, she has made an inference! To help other students understand the thought process behind the inference, then ask the student to support her comment with examples from the illustrations or text. Students may use picture clues, descriptions, or a character's thoughts, actions, or words as evidence.

See the box for additional prompts to help students make inferences.

The chart below was created by second graders for Big Anthony from *Strega Nona*.

Prompts for Inferring

✷ What is the setting of the story? How do you know? How does the author tell you without actually saying it was at the beach or in the forest? (A big wave rolled across the sand, soaking Jamie's towel— he is at the beach! How do you KNOW if the author did not say "beach"?)

✷ How did the character feel about _____? How do you know? What does he say or do that tells you he is angry or happy or sad? "Tommy slammed the door and stomped down the stairs of the apartment. He didn't even slow down when he heard his mother call him from the upstairs window." How can you tell he is angry if the author never says that word?

✷ The story doesn't say what happened next. What do you think would have happened if the author had added another chapter? Why do you think that? What told you that they lived happily ever after?

Strega Nona, by Tomie dePaola

Big Anthony

Looks Like	Character Traits
brown hair	careless
tall	tries hard
young	doesn't listen
thin	disrespectful
freckles	rude
wears a hat	

After five or six characteristics are listed in each column, fold the chart in half so that the physical characteristics are hidden and students can focus on the character traits. Ask them to complete the following sentence:

I think _____ was _____, because _____.
　　　　[character]　　　[character trait]　　　[support from text]

Encourage students to add as many examples and as much information as they can to support their inference. When they say, "I think Big Anthony was careless," they are making an inference; when they add, "I think Big Anthony was careless, because he didn't listen to Strega Nona" they are supporting that inference. If they can then supply a specific example (see student sample), they are learning to fully develop their inferential thinking.

Student Samples

I think Big Anthony was careless, because he didn't listen to Strega Nona. He only heard part of what she said and didn't know how to stop the pot from boiling. He made a mess, because he was careless.

I think the Cat in the Hat was clever, because he could think of all kinds of good tricks. He talked in rhymes when he talked.

I think the Cat in the Hat was messy, because he spilled the milk and ruined the cake. He messed up the whole house.

Tip It's important to carry out this activity with familiar stories, picture books, or fairy tales because the stories' characters usually have obvious personality traits that jump out at the reader. Often characters in basal readers are not as easy to evaluate, because they're usually more bland.

Follow-up Ideas . . . .

Students can complete this exercise in their journals as a literature-response activity to an independent-reading book.

Writing on an Assigned Topic

Skill Focus: *Responding to a Prompt*

CONNECTION TO WRITING ASSESSMENTS . . . .

❋ Introduces writing prompts.

❋ Provides practice with graphic organizers.

Though first graders and beginning second graders are often perceived as too young for report writing, my experience has convinced me otherwise. Report writing in these early grades is usually successful at the end of a unit, as children then have several concrete experiences to write about.

The students who wrote the sample below had just completed a unit on pets and were assigned to write an essay about a pet they have or wished they could have. I asked them to include specific information in their essay and presented them with the following assignment.

The Assignment

Topic: Write about a pet you have or would like to have. Be sure to answer these questions in your report:

1. What kind of food does it eat?

2. What trick can it do?

3. Where does the pet sleep?

This activity is designed for students in the second grade, but often students as young as kindergarten are ready to write such reports. It is also appropriate for third graders if they have not yet had success learning to write meaningful sentences about their experiences.

Defining Our Terms

Sometimes students will ask me what the difference between a report, an essay, and a story is. Here's how I define them: An essay is something that comes from the mind of the student. You can write an essay on why you like school or what you want to be when you grow up.

A *report* is more factual. You would write a report about bees or how to take care of a pet. In a report you are using your own words to say something you have learned through experience or research.

A *story* is a retelling of a fiction or nonfiction event, and often involves revealing emotions and wishes.

Presenting the Lesson

After the class has completed a unit of study by way of a variety of activities (see box), announce that everyone will write a report to sum up the unit.

Begin by reviewing the unit: Spend 20 minutes looking at bulletin boards and posters, rereading charts and graphs, recapping information learned from books, experiments, displays, or field trips, and from discussing student projects.

Unit Activities
Reading books.
Listening to "above reading level" books read aloud.
Watching a video.
Performing a science experiment.
Completing an art project.
Creating a bulletin board.
Playing a "Jeopardy" game of unit facts.
Going on a field trip.

PREPARATION:
Complete a unit of study on almost any topic. Animals are particularly easy, because students like them and there is abundant reading material at the lower grade levels on this subject.

TIME ALLOTTED:
30 to 45 minutes.

MATERIALS:
Chart paper and markers; writing and drawing paper, pencils, and colored pencils or crayons. (Students may also use Alpha Smarts or Dreamwriters.)

Following that, ask students to fold a sheet of paper into quarters and then open it and lay it flat. (Model this if they've had limited practice with graphic organizers.) Show how to number the boxes 1 through 4, beginning in the upper left-hand corner.

Indicating the upper left-hand box, ask the class to draw a picture of the topic (for example, the kind of pet they have or would like). This focuses them on the subject of the report and may provide information for the introduction. In the next three boxes, they should illustrate responses to the three questions their report has to answer. (For example, the pet's food, what trick it can do, and where the pet sleeps.)

Next, students can begin writing their reports. Since they often have trouble getting started, it's helpful to offer a suggestion on how to begin. For the pet report, I asked students to look at their picture and imagine the sound their animal makes. If they didn't know how to spell the sound, I told them to just guess. If their animal didn't make a sound (such as a snail), I challenged them to think of a describing word related to the animal and how it moves (Slime, slide.) This strategy got students going and introduced them to a neat way to begin a piece of writing—onomatopoeia. As always, I wrote along with my students on chart paper, providing a model for them to consult.

Next, ask students to read the first question, which prompts them to write their second sentence. Ask several students to share what they will write, and help any students who are having trouble deciding what to say. Some kids now will be off and running, easily answering the remaining questions and writing sentences based on their graphic organizers. Others may still be ruminating on the sound word. This is okay. Students who finish first can proofread their stories, embellish the illustrations, even add extensions to the text. (Remind everyone to end their report with a sentence that sums up their feelings—for example, "I love my gerbil!" or "I hope I can get a bird.") Meanwhile, complete your model essay (which matches the reproducible) on chart paper and circulate to help those moving more slowly. The least-experienced writers may copy much of your model essay, just inserting words that will make it fit their animal.

Morgan has illustrated pictures of her bird, what trick it can do, what it eats and where it likes to sleep.

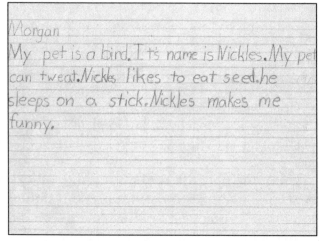

Morgan has successfully written six sentences about her bird.

Follow-up Ideas

Ask students to edit their essays by adding at least one extension sentence. They may either simply add a caret (^) and write in the sentence, or cut the paper apart and tape in blank paper on which to write more. For example, "I would feed it every day" and "I would give it a dish of milk."

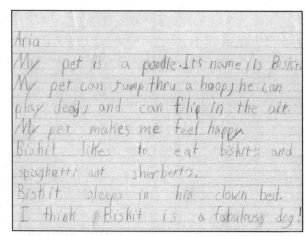

Aria has extended her story by listing several tricks her dog can do and various food it likes to eat.

Variations

Use the same report format for topics of study. For example, in a social studies lesson on Christopher Columbus. Have students begin the essay by imagining an expression Columbus might have used when he was sailing to America. Then provide three more pieces of information such as why he came here, what he found, and one more interesting fact. End with "Columbus was a famous explorer!" or a variation of that sentence. Remember to begin with the "graphic" graphic organizer!

Example #1

"Land, Ho!" yelled Christopher Columbus! He was looking for China. He found a new world. He called the people Indians. Columbus was a famous explorer.

Example #2

"Swab that deck, mate!" said Christopher Columbus. He had three ships. He found islands. He wanted to be rich. Columbus was famous for discovering America.

There are several interesting ways to end an essay. One is to repeat the sound or quotation from the introduction. Another is to ask the reader a question. Students might also want to expand the idea of circle writing from using just a word that was in the introduction to using a whole idea or phrase.

For a report on volcanoes the teacher might expect the child to tell three things they have learned about this subject. (The requirements, or assignments, do not always have to be specific questions!)

Example #1

A volcano is a mountain that explodes. The lava covers the land. The dust fills the air. A volcano can make an island. "Boom!" There goes another volcano.

Example #2

Special rocks come from volcanoes. They come out when the volcano explodes. The rocks are called lava. They are red hot and melted. When they cool off, the rocks are black. Have you ever seen a lava rock?

Extending and Developing an Essay

Skill Focus: *Adding Extensions*

CONNECTION TO WRITING ASSESSMENTS . . . .

❋ Using graphic organizers.

❋ Revising to develop ideas.

❋ Editing.

As a teacher, I find myself wanting to stretch my students and help them advance to the next level of achievement. I try to remember, however, that students often need extra practice at their current level to internalize concepts and build confidence before facing a new challenge. How do you tell if students are ready to learn about extending and developing a story or essay? If the majority of the class is automatically writing an introduction, a body including three details or facts, and has the ability to edit a closing (to go back to their writing and insert descriptive words, to erase a boring word and add a better one, to self-correct for meaning), then it's time. If most of the students cannot do all of this, do not move on to this lesson. (Most students remain at the five-to-eight sentence level throughout much of second grade.)

But if students seem bored with the simple writing activities outlined in previous lessons, or you sense that they have far more to say, try this activity on adding elaboration paragraphs, called "star paragraphs" for children. In an essay, a "star paragraph" (formally called an elaboration) is actually a complete paragraph that is intended to give a specific example, provide a short vignette, or clarify or describe something in great in detail. On most state writing assessments, this special paragraph can lift a score one whole level, but remember that students must have a firm foundation on which to build this new concept. The examples presented here are on a second-grade level and are not "scorable" by most state standards and therefore would NOT necessarily raise the score of a FOURTH-grade essay.

PREPARATION:
Present this lesson after an exciting event in class or at the end of a unit of study so that students have a good understanding of the subject matter as well as a variety of charts, displays, posters, and so on around the room. Briefly review appropriate terms and vocabulary before beginning.

TIME ALLOTTED:
Three or four 45-minute writing sessions, depending on the students' ability level.

MATERIALS:
Student writing and drawing materials, teacher modeling materials.

Presenting the Lesson

DAY ONE

Choose a topic for the whole class to write about: best friends, a favorite television show, getting new shoes, a cool day at school, fun on the playground, or a favorite food.

In the example that follows, I asked children to write about a good friend. I began by discussing the qualities of a best friend and asking why students might choose a particular person to be a friend. (Their responses included: "We play together"…"share things"… "go to the same church"… "live in the same neighborhood"… "like to dress alike"… "are on the same sports team.")

Then ask children to fold a piece of drawing paper into four sections, creating a graphic organizer to guide their writing. In the upper left-hand corner, they should draw a picture of the general topic. In my example they drew a picture of their best friend. In the other three boxes, they illustrated three reasons this person was their friend. One graphic organizer showed two boys in the same scout uniform, two houses side by side to indicate that they live in the same neighborhood, and two glasses of Slurpees, indicating that the boys liked to go to 7-11 together.

DAY TWO

After completing their graphic organizers, ask students to copy your introduction on writing paper. Again, from my example, the introductory sentence began:

My best friend is _____

Next, the children should complete three sentences, making sure they echo the illustrations. For example:

I am _____'s friend, because _____

The student should complete this sentence and add at least one more on the same topic.

We can _____

The child might try to think of things they can do together such as ride bikes or earn scout badges. After stating that, he should add a second, supporting sentence, an extension, about that activity.

We also like to _____.

> *The child would tell about things that he and his friend like to do together. He would also include a second or third extension, or supporting sentence giving a detail of this activity.*

> *For a closing, instruct the students to try to write in a circle and try to include an emotion word.*

For example:

_____ makes me feel _____.

> *Here, a second sentence is optional. At this level of writing, we permit introductions and closings to be only one sentence long. That is not usually the case at the fourth-grade level.*

Students should add a title last, when the essay is complete.

END OF DAY TWO OR START OF DAY THREE

Ask students to revise their essays using the following technique, called R.E.A.D.:

1. R — REREAD

Have students reread their essays by pointing to every word and slowly reading out loud. (The classroom will be noisy, but it only lasts for a moment!) Allow students to make corrections in their writing. Take a minute for students to tell what their error was: "I wrote 'the the'" or "I left the 's' off of puzzles!" This helps the rest of the class to hear what kind of mistakes to look for and also helps them to realize that it is natural and common to make these kinds of errors.

2. E — ERASE

Ask students to look for boring words such as *fun* or *good*. Allow students to erase these words and change them to more exciting words such as *exciting* or *delicious*.

3. A — ADD

In this step, students are encouraged to use a caret (^) to insert words to make their writing come alive. They naturally will want to add adjectives (the BIG tree; the YELLOW cat), but also ask them to put in adverbs and similes. ("He guarded our house 'like a soldier.'" or "He walked slowly out of the door.")

4. D — DID

This refers to writing in a circle, which has been discussed throughout this book. The fourth step of the revising process reminds the child to ask "DID I write in a circle?" The child should choose one word, phrase or idea from the introduction and include it in the closing. This makes the essay, story or report seem "whole and complete," which are valuable writing characteristics.

DAY THREE

For the "star paragraph" (or elaboration paragraph), ask students to choose one paragraph from their just-completed essay and cut their paper apart just as that paragraph ends. Tape in some additional lines of paper (about three or four) or paste this onto a new sheet of writing paper so that the child will have additional space to add a new paragraph.

Then ask the child to print the words "One time" to begin the new paragraph. The child should then write to tell an event that happened "one time" when they were doing something. For example, if she wrote, "We also like to play hopscotch." The "One time…" paragraph might be: "One time we played all day long on Saturday. We played so long we almost forgot to eat lunch!"

Follow-up Ideas......

Building in a star paragraph is easy if students have completed essays in their portfolios. Ask them to choose one, cut it apart, and to tape on some additional paper on which they can write. Alternatives to a "One time…" example or elaboration to an essay include almost any transition phrase, but easy ones for children are: "I remember…," "Last week (month, year, holiday)…," and "Whenever…."

Logan uses an Alpha Smart computer to revise his story.

CHAPTER 5

Evaluating Student Work

One of the most difficult aspects of teaching writing is evaluating student work. Throughout the country, methods of grading writing vary widely, with some schools requiring teachers to give a simple "S" or "U" for Satisfactory or Unsatisfactory, to others requiring a range of letter or number grades indicating specific levels of proficiency. While grading is a tough problem for every writing teacher, it is even more difficult for teachers working with the youngest students.

This chapter presents three simple rubrics, each designed to easily assess writing samples in grades K-2. The skills evaluated range all the way from holding a writing implement correctly to adding extensions to topic sentences. They are quite specific in spelling out expectations for students at various grade levels. The rubrics are easy to use and can be adapted for letter or number grades for those of you who are required to use these reporting systems. Each rubric reflects skills that have been presented in this book and elements of writing that are scored on writing assessments in the fourth and fifth grade.

If necessary, use the chart on the following page for assigning letter grades.

Individual schools may choose to set their own guidelines for scoring student writing. They could choose to give more credit for including a period than for holding the implement correctly. It is important that teachers within a building agree on how to use these rubrics so that students within one neighborhood are evaluated using the same criteria.

Each rubric is divided into four sections and includes a suggestion for the kind of writing sample for which it is appropriate. A sound practice is to collect a writing sample from each child periodically throughout the year and to evaluate each with the same rubric. (I like to collect four samples altogether, and I evaluate each on the same rubric; that's why the enclosed rubrics are divided into four boxes.) Your evaluations will not only show the growth of a writer over the course of the year but also will be useful for parent conferences; as justification for retention or placement in a special class; or to provide information for next year's teacher. Ideally, this process would take place annually, and the three rubrics with accompanying writing samples would become a part of an academic portfolio to showcase student growth from kindergarten to grade two.

GRADE K–5

The 5 proficiencies can directly correspond with letter grades A–F. For example, if a teacher gives a student credit for all 5—it is an A; 4 areas is a B, etc.

GRADE 1 THROUGH MID GRADE 2

Here, a student is assessed on 6 areas of proficiency. A student needs credit for all 6 to receive an A; 5 for a B; 4 for a C; 3 for a D; 2 or 1 for an F.

FROM MID GRADE 2

There are 8 proficiences on which the student is assessed. Student papers can be scored as follows. Credit for 8 is an A; 7 or 6 is a B; 5 or 4 is a C; 3 is a D and below is an F.

Kindergarten Writing Rubric

Name _____ Date _____

First Semester_____

First Writing Sample: Printed name.

1. Holds writing implement correctly . . . . [ ]
2. Forms letters correctly . . . . [ ]

    circle/ball [ ]   lines top to bottom [ ]

3. Writes from left to right . . . . [ ]
4. Spells name correctly . . . . [ ]
5. Uses only one capital letter in name . . . . [ ]

Second Writing Sample: Printed name and printed name of a favorite book character.

1. Forms letters correctly . . . . [ ]

    circle/ball [ ]   lines top to bottom [ ]

2. Writes from left to right . . . . [ ]
3. Spells name and character name correctly . . . . [ ]
4. Uses capital letters to begin names . . . . [ ]
5. Make letters one and two spaces high . . . . [ ]

Second Semester_____

Third Writing Sample: Printed name plus one short sentence copied from a chart.

1. Forms letters correctly . . . . [ ]
2. Writes from left to right and from top to bottom of page . . . . [ ]
3. Uses both uppercase and lowercase letters . . . . [ ]
4. Separates words with spaces . . . . [ ]
5. Includes a period . . . . [ ]

Fourth Writing Sample: Printed name plus one short sentence copied from a chart with a personal word added.

1. Forms letters correctly . . . . [ ]
2. Uses capital letters where appropriate . . . . [ ]
3. Separates words with spaces . . . . [ ]
4. Includes a period . . . . [ ]
5. Selects and prints an appropriate personal word . . . . [ ]

Comments: _____

_____

_____

_____

First-Grade Writing Rubric

Name _____ Date _____

First Semester_____

Writing sample: Printed name plus one sentence copied from a chart.

1. Holds writing implement correctly . . . . ☐

2. Writes from left to right and from top to bottom of page . . . . ☐

3. Forms letters correctly . . . . ☐

4. Uses capital letters where appropriate . . . . ☐

5. Separates words with spaces . . . . ☐

6. Includes a period . . . . ☐

Writing sample: Printed name plus one sentence copied from a chart with one personal word added.

1. Selects and prints appropriate personal word . . . . ☐

2. Writes from left to right and from top to bottom of page . . . . ☐

3. Forms letters correctly . . . . ☐

4. Separates words with spaces . . . . ☐

5. Includes a period or other punctuation . . . . ☐

6. Uses capital letters where appropriate . . . . ☐

Second Semester_____

Writing sample: Printed name plus three sentences, at least one of which is original.

1. Original sentence contributes to the story line . . . . ☐

2. Writing sample contains at least three sentences . . . . ☐

3. Original sentence uses an emotion word or a descriptive word . . . . ☐

4. Separates words with spaces . . . . ☐

5. Includes periods or other punctuation . . . . ☐

6. Uses capital letters where appropriate . . . . ☐

Writing sample: Printed name plus at least three original sentences.

1. Sentences are all on the same topic . . . . ☐

2. Writing has an introduction, body, and closing . . . . ☐

3. Writing contains an emotion word or descriptive word . . . . ☐

4. One topic sentence has an extension . . . . ☐

5. Includes periods or other punctuation . . . . ☐

6. Uses capital letters where appropriate . . . . ☐

Comments: _____

_____

_____

15 Easy Lessons That Build Basic Writing Skills in Grades K-2 Scholastic Professional Books

Second-Grade Writing Rubric

Name _____ Date _____

First Semester_____

Writing sample: Name plus at least three original sentences.

   1. Sentences are all on the same topic . . . . ☐

   2. Story has an introduction, body, and closing. . . . . ☐

   3. Story contains an emotion or descriptive word or phrase. . . . . ☐

   4. One topic sentence has an extension. . . . . ☐

   5. Includes periods or other punctuation . . . . ☐

   6. Uses capital letters where appropriate . . . . ☐

Writing sample: Name plus at least five original sentences.

   1. Sentences are all on the same topic . . . . ☐

   2. Story has an introduction, body, and closing. . . . . ☐

   3. Writing contains emotion or descriptive words or phrases. . . . . ☐

   4. One topic sentence has an extension. . . . . ☐

   5. Includes periods or other punctuation . . . . ☐

   6. Uses capital letters where appropriate . . . . ☐

Second Semester_____

Writing sample: Name plus at least eight original sentences.

   1. Sentences are all on the assigned topic . . . . ☐

   2. Writing has an introduction, body, and closing. . . . . ☐

   3. Writing has at least three topic sentences . . . . ☐

   4. Writing contains at least two extensions . . . . ☐

   5. Writing contains emotion or descriptive words or phrases. . . . . ☐

   6. Includes periods or other punctuation . . . . ☐

   7. Uses capital letters where appropriate . . . . ☐

   8. Writing has reasonable spelling of second-grade level words . . . . ☐

Writing sample: Name plus at least eight original sentences.

   1. Sentences are all on the assigned topic . . . . ☐

   2. Writing has an introduction, body, and closing. . . . . ☐

   3. Writing has at least three topic sentences . . . . ☐

   4. Writing contains at least two extensions . . . . ☐

   5. Writing contains emotion or descriptive words or phrases. . . . . ☐

   6. Includes periods or other punctuation . . . . ☐

   7. Uses capital letters where appropriate . . . . ☐

   8. Story has reasonable spelling of second-grade level words . . . . ☐

Comments: _____

Name _____ Date _____

Title: _____

_____

- -

_____

- -

_____

- -

_____

- -

_____

- -

_____

- -

_____

- -

_____

- -

_____

- -

_____

15 Easy Lessons That Build Basic Writing Skills in Grades K-2 Scholastic Professional Books

Name _____

Date _____

Title: _____

Notes